HOMOSEXUAL
NO MORE

"Three years ago God answered my prayer for help when I started to work with Dr. Consiglio. He has helped me get in touch with root emotional issues and, as a result, I have experienced successively greater degrees of freedom from homosexual symptoms. Personal satisfaction and peace have increased to levels I never thought would be possible."

Bruce

"I've been married for two years now and I thank the Lord this has come about through Bill's ministry and counseling. I wouldn't have believed that the struggle with homosexuality could be such a remote part of my past as it is now."

Donald

"The Lord has done 'immeasurably more than I could ask or imagine' through Dr. Bill's counseling and HOPE Ministries. After two years of very painful ups and downs I am changing in so many ways. There really is hope for the homosexual."

Greg

HOMOSEXUAL NO MORE

DR. WILLIAM CONSIGLIO

VICTOR BOOKS®

A DIVISION OF SCRIPTURE PRESS PUBLICATIONS INC.
USA CANADA ENGLAND

Unless otherwise indicated, Scripture quotations are from the *Holy Bible, New International Version,* © 1973, 1978, 1984, International Bible Society. Used by permission of Zondervan Bible Publishers; other quotations are from the *Authorized (King James) Version* (KJV), the *New American Standard Bible* (NASB), © the Lockman Foundation 1960, 1962, 1963, 1968, 1971, 1972, 1973, 1975, 1977. Used by permission; and *The Living Bible* (TLB), © 1971, Tyndale House Publishers, Wheaton, IL 60189. Used by permission; the *Good News Bible* (GNB), © American Bible Society 1966, 1971, 1976; J.B. Phillips: *The New Testament in Modern English,* Revised Edition (PH), © J.B. Phillips, 1958, 1960, 1972, permission of Macmillan Publishing Co. and Collins Publishers.

Library of Congress Cataloging-in-Publication Data

Consiglio, William.
    Homosexual no more / William Consiglio.
      p.   cm.
    ISBN 0-89693-935-9
    1. Homosexuality—Religious aspects—Christianity. 2. Gays—Religious life.   I. Title.
BR115.H6C675   1991
208'.664—dc20   91-15467
                                         CIP

---

4   5   6   7   8   9   10   Printing/Year   95

CONTENTS

Introduction **9**

Chapter One
Reorientation Therapy:
A Way Out of Homosexuality **17**

Chapter Two
Answer These Four Questions:
Ten Facts about Homosexuality **27**

Chapter Three
All Things Work Together for Good:
Spiritual Renewal **43**

Chapter Four
I Never Chose to Be Homosexual **57**

Chapter Five
What Do I Have to Do to Change? **84**

Chapter Six
It Begins to Hurt—You Begin to Heal **100**

Chapter Seven
Putting Away Childish Things:
Conversations with God **118**

Chapter Eight
Conversations with the Inner Parent **134**

Chapter Nine
Train Up a Child:
Conversations with the Inner Child **152**

Chapter Ten
  In Due Season We Shall Reap:
  A Bible Study Summary **170**

Chapter Eleven
  Homosexual No More:
  David's Testimony **179**

Glossary of Terms **195**

Recommended Reading List **202**

To my wife Linda and my pastor Owen Sanderson
for their love and encouragement
To all those who are about to change,
let this be your prayer:

My hope is built on nothing less
Than Jesus' blood and righteousness.
No merit of my own I claim,
But wholly lean on Jesus' name.
On Christ, the solid Rock, I stand,
All other ground is sinking sand.

John Bacchus Dykes

INTRODUCTION:
The Inner World of Homosexuality

From the time you were very young you began to feel different. You were unsure of yourself; you were less confident than others; you were less assertive. You had fears and anxieties. You were very sensitive about things. What other boys brushed aside lightly seemed to bother and trouble you more deeply.

These emotional differences started to make you feel alone and very self-conscious. You started to compare yourself with others and found yourself falling short. You were self-critical, self-condemning, and self-judging. Perhaps you didn't feel worthwhile, significant, or really important to anyone. You felt like you were not understood or accepted and you started a life of hiding, pretending, denying, and covering up the real inside of you with a false, protective, and substitute self. As a result, you moved out of childhood with large parts of yourself buried, unsettled, or lost. Chronologically you continued to grow and change year after year, but emotionally you remained fixed and unfinished in childhood.

You especially felt shame. Shame is a feeling of being incomplete or having failed at being a person. It's a sense of yourself as not good enough or adequate. Shame tells you that you should be something better or different than who you are. Guilt is about something you did that was not acceptable. That's not the same as shame. Shame is about being unacceptable about who you are. All those feelings which were uncomfortable and unacceptable were really happening to you but you hid them from yourself. To hide them, to pretend that they don't exist, is to feel that **you** don't exist, because when we are children, we are what we feel. To invalidate your feelings is to say that you don't exist. You become a body; a shell without a self.

That sensitive inner child of feelings remains hurt and hidden in you even though you are now an adult. Your feelings often do not match your age. For instance, you came to criticize and dislike feelings like anger, fear, inadequacy, insecurity, and especially your sexual feelings. You don't trust them; they are too disturbing to you. You don't trust yourself and you don't let anyone else know who you really are. A full scale self-rejection began to take place. With it went your sense of yourself as a male; your gender security.

And so you became gender empty. As you get a little older, you start to notice something else which embarrasses you. You begin to have to admit to yourself that you're more curious and attracted to other males than the opposite sex. You like their attention. You like this one person's attention. You crave his interest. He intrigues you. You envy him and want to be like him. His attitudes, his behavior, his way of walking and talking and looking fascinates you. Now you even start to want a relationship with him; an intimacy with him. You are trying to re-create your lost self.

You are a little older and it's all becoming sexualized. You are surprised and excited when a same-sex person hugs you. A touch, a casual arm around the shoulder, a pat on the back is something that means a lot to you. Another same-sex person brushing up against you is noticed and makes you hungry for more contact; more intimacy and closeness. Nudity, pornography, lusting with your eyes, falling in love, getting emotionally attached, feeling jealous and empty without him; all these things start to preoccupy you.

Finally, you have to admit it. You have to say the words inside of yourself. "I'm homosexual." You begin to yield to these feelings and thoughts and desires, and maybe even begin to act on them. You experience a release, a relief. You break through a barrier. It's all so pervasive and powerful. How can you be any different? How can it change? How can you ever be happy without it? How can you deny what seems so needed, so natural, so important?

Yet, there is another all-pervasive and powerful experience in you. It is the wonderful presence of Jesus. He has come into your life, and you have entered His life and kingdom. Second Corinthians 5:17 happened to you. "Behold, if anyone is in Christ Jesus, he is a whole new creation. The old has to go, and all things are becoming new" (freely rendered).

You have been living in Romans 6–7 but He wants you in Romans 8. He makes you a promise: "No eye has seen, no ear has heard, no mind has conceived what God has prepared for those who love Him" (1 Cor. 2:9). You hear the Lord say to you, "Those whom I love, I rebuke and discipline. So be earnest and repent. To him who overcomes, I will give the right to sit with Me on My throne" (Rev. 3:19, 21). You are an overcomer—a person who wants to control and manage and overcome homosexuality or even recover your heterosexuality. You want to get into Romans 8 where all things start working together for good; where the law of the Spirit of life will set you free from the law of sin and death; where God is our Abba Father and we are heirs with Christ. You want to get into Romans 8 where He will give us all things and where nothing can separate us from the love of God. And that's why you are reading this book.

As you begin this book, I want to be honest and open with you. Ten years ago I knew virtually nothing about homosexuality. I also had the classic homophobic profile. I was uninformed, embarrassed, uncomfortable, and even a bit repulsed by homosexuality. As a Christian, I knew that I should love the sinner and hate the sin, but I honestly didn't want to love this kind of sinner. The homosexual feelings I myself felt when I was in an all-male seminary as a young man were embarrassing to me and like other males I would just as soon forget about them altogether. I was content that the Lord hadn't sent me such clients. But the Lord had different plans when He sent Jay to me.

Jay was completing his senior year of business school. A saved and committed biblical Christian, he was in pain about his homosexuality. He knew it was wrong and yet he was drawn into one emotional and sexual relationship after another. He wanted me to help him. Was there any hope for him, he asked. He was ambivalent about beginning counseling. There were no guarantees of success. Would things get better? What if this failed also? I also had a lot of doubts and reservations. Does he have to change? Does he really want to change? Can he change? How does change come about? What are realistic goals to achieve?

Later I got alone before the Lord in prayer. He reminded me of the Scriptures He had been teaching me to live by as a Christian counselor. " 'Not by might, not by power, but by My Spirit,' says the Lord of Hosts" (Zech. 4:6). "Behold, I am the Lord, the God of all flesh; is there anything too difficult for Me?" (Jer. 32:27) "For it is God who works in you to will and to act according to His good purpose" (Phil. 2:13). And especially that miracle verse which has seen me and others through hundreds of crises and problems and disappointments, "All things work together for good for the one who loves God and is called according to His purpose" (Rom. 8:28).

As He reminded me of these words I felt a tremendous desire to work with Jay. He also showed me that Jay began to develop the two things that produce miraculous changes in people's lives. Jay was forming a strong personal desire and commitment to change. He made a decision to change and was ready to stand by it. And second, he was developing a strong personal faith and trust in the Lord who he knew would produce this change in him. How about you? Do you really want to be made whole? Do you really believe and trust the Lord to do it?

These words from Scripture also made me feel that I had begun what would soon become the biggest challenge of my personal and professional life. I felt like some scientist who was on the horizon of a new discovery. More than that! I began to realize that this was a calling.

God was calling me to a spiritual work which He Himself had begun. This was not my work, but His. He began it because He loves to make His children whole. This was a ministry the Lord prepared for me. I must respond. "Therefore, since through God's mercy we have this ministry, we do not lose heart" (2 Cor. 4:1).

I worked with Jay for over a year. In that time I witnessed a miracle. He ended all homosexual behavior. But even more, he had experienced tremendous inner healing and renewal. He had grown in his self-esteem and self-image. Most amazingly, his heterosexuality had stirred in him. He became interested in women. "Lord," I hesitantly prayed, "You are wonderful. How glorious are Your ways. Now, Lord, I have a little request; would You just send me one more person to see if You and I can do it again?" That was ten years ago. Almost 100 clients later I have seen the Lord continue to perform the miracle of transformed lives. That's what this book is about.

Are you feeling encouraged by what I've said? Go ahead! Allow yourself to feel hopeful. You can let the desire for change really begin to soar in your spirit. It's from the Lord. At the same time, let me ask the question that may be on your mind. Does that mean that everyone should expect a complete heterosexual recovery? No! Every person is different. People are complex and human sexuality is one of the most complex aspects of human personality to work with. And yet, this book does give evidence that many can make substantial heterosexual recovery. You may be one of those people. It is also a testimony to the fact that a number of others achieve a significant degree of emotional healing, growth in self-esteem, and spiritual well being and are able to move on in life freed of the homosexual obsession and preoccupation. It allows them to form rewarding and fulfilling relationships and live more integrated and satisfying lives which are compatible with their spiritual values and convictions. And that's powerfully good news in itself.

I also have a word for you who are counseling overcomers. I began to ask the Lord, "Why me? Why did You select me to do this kind of work?" Over time He answered that question by showing me what I had to bring to this work that He can use to heal people. Some of it was pleasant to see; some was not. If you are doing this work, don't only look at what is most effective about yourself; be sure to look at what is most weak also. The Lord uses both. I have found a secret of the Christian life to be that we must take everything that we are, the strong and the broken, the weak and the unfinished, and let the Lord put it to use. Overcomers need to realize that the Lord can use their homosexual struggle to bless them and others if they will give it to Him for His use.

In my work with overcomers the Lord uses my background from a family with certain dysfunctional aspects. My family, so culturally rich and special in many ways, also left me confused about my gender security and my emotional self for a part of the first twenty-five years of my life. I had to do some personal growing myself, and though I never got into homosexuality, my emotional background gave me a sensitivity for people who hurt in this way. I know it had much to do with my decision to become a therapist.

I'm also a person with a lot of optimism and I can create hope in others. That's important for overcomers. I like to deeply listen to people. I like to nurture people and see them grow. I'm very persevering and patient. I'm not afraid to show my love to other men, verbally and physically. Coming from an effusive Italian family, touching, holding, and hugging are comfortable for me. This can be troublesome as well as useful with overcomers, so we need to discern the use of it wisely.

But perhaps the biggest reason the Lord led me to this work is because ministry is always mutual. The Lord always calls a person to a ministry that will bless and heal him as well as those he serves. I have experienced much growth through doing this work, and I praise God for it with all my heart. God continues to choose the foolish things and the weak things to do His work. He continues to select those who are only vessels of clay to show that the power for healing is from Him and not ourselves.

If you are a pastor or counselor, or especially if you are a Christian who is an overcomer yourself working with other overcomers, I encourage you to turn to these Scriptures and meditate on them as you begin this book. Go back to them often. They will help you maintain dignity, propriety, balance, and purpose. Psalm 69:5-6; Ezekiel 34; Acts 20:28; 2 Corinthians 4; Philippians 2:13; Hebrews 6:10-12; 13:20-21; James 5:19-20; 1 Peter 5:2-4.

This book evolved from ten years of experience with overcomers. I thank each one of them. They allowed me to learn from them. They showed me how the truth really sets you free. I feel a special gratitude to Dr. Elizabeth Moberly whom the Lord brought into my life at just the right time. She gave me the encouragement I sorely needed. I thank her for helping me enter the world of publishing. I also thank Bob Davies of Exodus who gave the manuscript a thorough scrutiny. He helped me to tidy up wording which was either unclear or unnecessary. This last year was the most rewarding, largely due to Greg Clouse and Barbara Williams. Their kindness, helpfulness, and expertise blessed me so much. Thank you, and thank all of you behind the scenes at Victor Books.

CHAPTER ONE

REORIENTATION THERAPY: A WAY OUT OF HOMOSEXUALITY

Rick* admitted that he had considered suicide after his last lover left him. He was desperate and hurt. He had "come out" into an active homosexual lifestyle three years ago when he was 23. He had had several short-lived relationships and encounters during that time. The last relationship with Ray seemed so promising. Ray was "Mr. Right." They had a lot in common and really seemed to care for each other. There was that initial excitement and "high" from being with someone you are attracted to and want to be with all the time. Ray treated Rick as if he were someone very special.

Everything went well for the first three months. Then there were the same signs Rick had seen develop in other relationships. Rick started to feel jealous every time Ray noticed another guy. He wanted Ray's exclusive attention and became irritated whenever Ray pointed out Rick's shortcomings.

Finally the day came when Ray said he was moving out. A heated argument developed and Ray admitted that he was interested in someone else. When he finally moved out, Rick cried for three straight nights. "I got so depressed," Rick said, "that I didn't want to live anymore. That's when I started drinking heavily. I also began to have anxiety attacks and my doctor diagnosed the beginning of an ulcer." Rick would

*All names have been changed.

get drunk at night in order to fall asleep, which made it difficult to concentrate at work.

It was around this time that Rick saw an ad in the newspaper for a ministry to Christians who desire to overcome homosexuality. "I saw ads like that before," Rick said, "but I always dismissed them as a lot of religious fanaticism. I had read so much about homosexuality that convinced me it was something you could not change. I had resigned myself to having been born homosexual and felt some peace from accepting myself as gay.

"I cut out the ad and tucked it in my wallet and forgot all about it. I remained miserable and depressed without Ray. I guess I was so desperate that when a female friend of mine invited me to go to an evening church service with her one night, I went along just so I would not be alone again. Being by myself in the evenings was starting to frighten me because I was thinking about suicide more and more."

That was the night Rick met Jesus Christ. In despair he had gone up to the altar to accept Christ into his life. "A great feeling of strength and peace came over me. I felt like I had been embraced by a powerful man who just held me and held me.

"The next day I took the ad from my wallet and called HOPE Ministries. Bill spoke to me for over an hour. It was such a relief just to talk and share my pain with someone who listened and seemed to care. At the end we prayed. I really didn't know how to pray out loud, but Bill's prayer gave me a feeling of strength, and for the first time, hope."

The pamphlet Rick received in the mail from HOPE Ministries said, "Commit thy way unto the Lord, trust also in Him; and He shall bring it to pass" (Ps. 37:5, KJV). Rick had prayed for instant healing from homosexuality in the past, as so many do, saying in effect what he had read in the Bible, "For this thing I besought the Lord thrice, that it might depart from me," and now God seemed to be answering him with the words from the rest of this verse, "And He said unto me, My grace is sufficient for thee: for My strength is made perfect in weakness" (2 Cor. 12:8-9, KJV).

Rick was beginning to turn his struggles over to the Lord, trusting what Jesus had said to the blind men,

"Believe ye that I am able to do this?" They said,
"Yea Lord." Then touched He their eyes, saying,
"According to your faith be it done unto you"
(Matt. 9:28-29, KJV).

The Lord led Rick, like countless others, to an ex-gay
ministry. HOPE Ministries of Connecticut Inc. is one of a
number of ministries springing up throughout the U.S. which
are helping single and married men and women who desire to
be delivered from homosexual feelings, thinking, and behavior. Combining education, emotional support, and counseling,
HOPE is an acronym for Honesty, Openness, Prayer, and
Encouragement. Meeting weekly, this Christian fellowship
provides a safe and confidential place where people can share
their struggle; where they don't have to be alone with the
homosexual burden anymore; and where self-rejection and
pain can stop for a while. People gain support in being honest
with themselves and open with others, and that helps to
reduce the feelings of being alone, different, and isolated.
There, in prayer together, a person doesn't have to hide his
real fears and shame. He leaves with strength and encouragement to continue the process of change. His or her hope is
renewed.

When Rick came face-to-face with Jesus Christ, the initial
break with the homosexual bondage took place. As he continues to go to the HOPE Ministry meetings and receives the
strength and power of the Holy Spirit, he is beginning to see
the homosexual feelings fade and a new identity in Christ as a
whole man emerge. What the Bible says is true for Rick,
"When someone becomes a Christian he becomes a brand-
new person inside. He is not the same anymore. A new life
has begun" (2 Cor. 5:17, TLB).

OVERCOMERS

Rick is an overcomer, and this is a book for people who are
overcomers and for those who want to help overcomers. An
overcomer is a Christian man or woman who, for personal
and moral reasons, is overcoming homosexual feelings,
thoughts, desires, attractions, behavior-orientation, or lifestyle.

I have been engaged in the counseling of some 70 or 80 overcomers and have worked with some 500 or more overcomers, pastors, counselors, family, and friends of overcomers through our group ministry. This book is meant to bring together some of the most useful information, suggestions, and practical strategies which I have developed and used with demonstrated success over the last several years.

I call my approach to working with overcomers **Reorientation Therapy.** The term comes from a simple analogy which I have often used to explain my view of the development of homosexuality.

THE STREAM OF SEXUALITY

This can be illustrated if we picture human sexuality as a stream or river (see diagram #1). There is only one stream of sexuality as God designed it. That stream is a heterosexual stream. God created all people heterosexual.

Diagram 1

The Stream of Sexuality

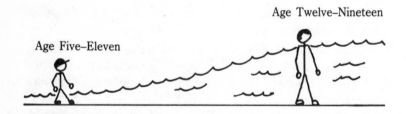

Age Twelve–Nineteen

Age Five–Eleven

Picture a child somewhere between age five through eleven standing in that stream of heterosexuality. At this preadolescent time of human sexual development, picture the **cool** waters of sexuality flowing **gently** by at about the height of his **ankles.** In this period of childhood, sexuality is cool (i.e., not very pleasurable); it flows gently (i.e., not very powerful); and it is only at ankle height (i.e., not very pervasive).

But now picture the adolescent, age twelve through nineteen. In adolescence the stream of sexuality has become a **hot** (i.e., very pleasurable), and **very rapid** (i.e., very powerful) river which is at the height of his **chin** (i.e., very pervasive). For the rest of adulthood sexuality is a very powerful, pervasive, and pleasurable force in a person's life. As adults, the fact is, we are all very sexual people.

Diagram 2

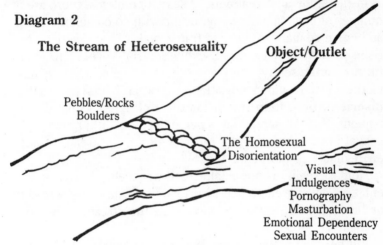

The Stream of Heterosexuality

Object/Outlet

Pebbles/Rocks
Boulders

The Homosexual
Disorientation

Visual
Indulgences
Pornography
Masturbation
Emotional Dependency
Sexual Encounters

Now picture that stream again (see diagram #2). When we see human sexuality as a stream, it helps us to understand a number of realities about human sexuality and the development of homosexuality.

First, it is important to repeat that the stream of sexuality is designed by God as a heterosexual one only. Therefore, human sexuality has as its outlet, physical, emotional, and spiritual bonding with the opposite sex.

Secondly, human sexuality is a powerful force that is always flowing. You can't stop a flowing stream of water. If you block it with pebbles, rocks, or boulders, it will find a way over or around the blockages and continue to flow. Another stream or several streams will start to form as a result of these blockages. As a child I would play on a beach by making lines in the sand which would fill with water from the ocean tide. If I blocked those streams with pebbles, the strong rush of the next wave would cause the water to overflow and form another stream.

Human sexuality is like that. It is a powerful force which

will always be active and find expression in one form or another. If the stream of human heterosexuality is blocked in childhood or adolescence, it will likely form other streams (deviations or disorientations) off of the mainstream. And so, in spite of these blockages, it will find some form of expression.

In the study and treatment of sexual problems, there are a number of deviations that can occur with so complex a thing as human sexuality. There is transexuality, transvestism, fetishism, sadism, masochism, exhibitionism, voyeurism, prostitution, promiscuity, and many others. Homosexuality is one of the most common deviations, or what I prefer to call a **disorientation,** from the mainstream of heterosexual development. It is not something a person is born with; rather, it is sexual disorientation when the God-designed stream of heterosexuality is blocked.

Homosexuality is not an alternative sexuality or sexual orientation, but an emotional disorientation caused by arrested or blocked emotional development in the stream of heterosexuality.

But here is the good news. When these pebbles, rocks, and boulders are successfully reduced, diminished, or removed, human sexuality can resume its natural heterosexual flow toward its proper, God-designed outlet; i.e., wholesome, mature, sexual, and emotional expression in marriage with a person of the opposite sex.

Reorientation therapy is an approach to helping overcomers remove the emotional, homosexual outlets which have become habitual.

What are some of those pebbles, rocks, and boulders? The pebbles and rocks blocking the stream are unresolved family/parental relationships, the lack of good peer relationships, ineffective techniques for dealing with temptation, the lack of understanding about homosexuality, and others. Some of the boulders are low self-esteem (LSE), gender emptiness (GE), negative interior conversations, a wounded area of emotions (deprivation complex), spiritual devitalization, and opposite sex intimacy anxiety.

The external behavioral outlets that continue to reinforce homosexuality must be diminished and eliminated. There are basically five: sexual encounters, emotional dependencies, masturbation, pornography, and visual indulgence or lust.

AN OVERVIEW

In the chapters ahead, you will see a planned, systematic approach to sexual reorientation which I've used with many overcomers. In the next three chapters I develop the foundation of personal motivation, spiritual strength, and an understanding of homosexual development which are needed to begin this journey of healing and recovery.

In chapter 2 there are four questions and ten facts about homosexuality which the overcomer (and the counselor) must resolve if he is to begin to get well. Chapter 3 provides the overcomer with the spiritual foundation and strength he will need through a changed heart and a personal relationship with the Lord Jesus Christ. In chapter 4 he learns how homosexuality developed in him through his family life. He is asked to trace the six stages of homosexuality as he looks at the life of another overcomer.

In chapters 5 through 9 I introduce the external and internal changes which heal homosexuality. Chapter 5 examines the seven personal and seven relational areas which make up the external changes of healing. Chapter 6 looks at the structure of the homosexual personality, the wounded area of fifteen emotions or needles which keep homosexuality alive, and the three inner conversations that need changing. (The first interior conversation [chapter 7] which begins the "transforming of the mind" is his conversations with God. Here the homosexual learns the ways in which he has distorted God through his father filter.)

Chapter 8 examines how the homosexual makes a number of "transferences" with people which make up the conversation he has with his critical inner parent. Chapter 9 explores the importance of emotional renewal as the overcomer changes the voice of his sensitive inner child.

Chapter 10 presents a practical plan of action based on a Bible study of Matthew 21:23-32. Here he learns that he can substantially accelerate his own healing when he learns to do daily self-therapy. The last chapter is a testimony by David describing his own recovery from homosexuality as he applied the principles and strategies of reorientation therapy to his life.

ARE YOU AN OVERCOMER?

You must begin with the conviction that homosexuality can be overcome, just as Rick is overcoming homosexuality. If you are a new creation in Christ, and the Spirit of Christ dwells within you, it is because God has poured the love of Christ into your heart and, "Who shall separate us from the love of Christ?" (Rom. 8:35, KJV) "To him that overcomes," says Christ, "I will grant him the right to sit with Me on My throne, even as I also overcame" (Rev. 3:21, KJV).

Christ's love working in you will not only help you overcome homosexuality, but will cause you to grow in a hundred ways. You are an overcomer. According to Les Carter you belong to

> A special class of individuals (which) distinguishes itself by a refusal to be held down by negative circumstances. (They) . . . are determined to grow in spite of adversity; they are not martyrs or nailtough stoics. They are realists who have willfully chosen to make responsible decisions even though they have been exposed to unfair circumstances and unwarranted difficulties. They are overcomers.[1]

What about you? Are you this kind of person? This quote suggests four important questions you need to ask yourself about your personal motivation for overcoming homosexuality. These questions entail ten important fundamental facts about homosexuality for the Christian overcomer. I invite you to really wrestle with these questions and facts. Talk them out with yourself sincerely and honestly. Talk them out with your counselor or others openly. They are very important, and you need to come to grips with them at the very beginning.

FOR THE COUNSELOR

As you embark on this work with your overcomer, you are entering a complex emotional, psychological, and spiritual journey of healing. You need the armor of God to protect yourself from the enemy's attacks. Remember, you are rescuing a child of God from the darkness which Satan has cast upon his life. Therefore, you should spend time in prayer.

From time to time you will notice that your overcomer seems caught up in discouragement, compulsiveness, lust, self-pity, emptiness, impulsiveness, loneliness, suicidal thoughts, anger, or fear. If you listen attentively and discerningly, you will sense when these attitudes trouble him. As you sense these things, pray a commanding prayer in the name of Jesus to free him from these overwhelming emotional and spiritual influences.

Take some time to understand this chapter. It provides you with an overview of where you are going. It acts as a sort of map for the journey. Your overcomer will need to rely on you for direction and guidance. He will need you to keep a clear vision of where he is going and what he is accomplishing. Therefore, review the chapters ahead. Get a sense of the whole framework of reorientation therapy. Diagram #3 provides a schematic of this framework.

Diagram 3   Framework of Reorientation Therapy

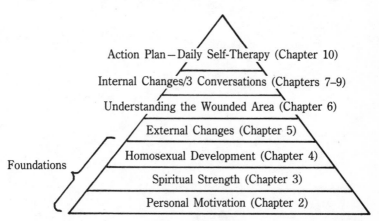

Action Plan—Daily Self-Therapy (Chapter 10)

Internal Changes/3 Conversations (Chapters 7–9)

Understanding the Wounded Area (Chapter 6)

External Changes (Chapter 5)

Homosexual Development (Chapter 4)

Spiritual Strength (Chapter 3)

Personal Motivation (Chapter 2)

Foundations

Do you understand these central elements of reorientation therapy? What goals does your overcomer seek? What goals do you seek? Can you identify the internal and external areas needing change? How will you monitor the five outlets of homosexuality?

Lastly, may I suggest that you keep written notes on each counseling session with your overcomer. In doing this you will be able to capture the central and recurring themes, data, and concerns of your overcomer. I even suggest that you tape your first session and other sessions (with your overcomer's permission) and spend time listening to them. Again, this is a helpful way of coming to an understanding of your overcomer as a person. Listen closely, under the Spirit's guidance, to understand what God reveals to you about him and the way in which the Lord wants you to work with him. Believe that God has sent this person to you, and that the Lord will use you in specific ways to heal your overcomer. " 'Not by might, nor by power, but by My Spirit,' saith the Lord of hosts" (Zech. 4:6, KJV).

---

1. Les Carter, *Putting the Past Behind* (Chicago: Moody Press, 1989), 115.

CHAPTER TWO

ANSWER THESE FOUR QUESTIONS: TEN FACTS ABOUT HOMOSEXUALITY

QUESTION ONE:
DO YOU KNOW THAT YOU HAVE TO CHANGE?
What makes your overcomer a part of a special class of individuals? The basic difference between him and the people living a gay lifestyle is that he knows he has to change. This is the bottom line. He has to change! And he is ready to take advantage of the grace which God desires to pour out on him as he begins this journey of healing.

Change is not an option! Therefore, fact number one is: God calls homosexual behavior SIN, and the overcomer must work to change this behavior and orientation. But wait a minute; ask your overcomer if he is certain about his need to change. Don't take it for granted that he has settled this issue just because he is a Christian. Is he certain of this? Look at God's Word together with him.

> Do you not know that the wicked will not inherit the kingdom of God? Do not be deceived: Neither the sexually immoral nor idolaters nor adulterers nor male prostitutes nor homosexual offenders . . . will inherit the kingdom of God. And that is what some of you were. But you were washed, you were sanctified, you were justified in the name of the Lord Jesus Christ and by the Spirit of our God (1 Cor. 6:9-11).

and,

> Even their women exchanged natural relations for
> unnatural ones. In the same way the men also
> abandoned natural relations with women and were
> inflamed with lust for one another. Men committed
> indecent acts with other men, and received in
> themselves the due penalty for their perversion
> (Rom. 1:26-27).

To an unsaved person, these words from the Bible are only
platitudes. But to the person who is reborn spiritually by the
Holy Spirit, indulging in homosexual thoughts, desires, and
behavior is sinful. The unsaved person, even if he calls himself a Christian, will deny the sinfulness of homosexuality and
will rationalize and justify himself in all kinds of ways in order
to engage in his fleshly pleasure or maintain his emotional
dependency and romantic ties to another same-sex person.
He does this because, "Unless a man is born again he cannot
see the kingdom of heaven" (John 3:3), for what is only
"flesh, gives birth to flesh; but the Spirit gives birth to the
Spirit" (John 3:6).

The passage in 1 Corinthians 6:9-11 makes two things
abundantly clear. First, people who continue to live a homosexual way of life cannot enter into that vital and personal
relationship with God or have God reigning in their hearts.
They will continue to distance themselves from God. No
amount of rationalizing or permissive interpretation of biblical
texts will change God's Word. A person who continues in
homosexuality will be out of fellowship with God. Homosexual behavior is sin because God's Word says so.

The good news comes in verse 11 where it says, "That is
what some of you **were**." This clearly means that change
happened to those homosexual Corinthians and that change is
possible. Change is a reality because God's Word says so.

Again, John says, "When the Holy Spirit comes, He will
convict the world of sin, of what is right living, and of judgment" (John 16:8).

The reborn Christian has received the Holy Spirit and the
Spirit has drawn a line across his heart; a line between what

is right and wrong. He now has an internal conviction that homosexuality is wrong, even though he may still be struggling with strong feelings, desires, and temptations. No amount of arguing will convince an unregenerate gay person of the sinfulness of homosexuality. I stopped doing this a long time ago. Now, all I do is present the Word of God and let the Holy Spirit do the convicting work. All I can do is plant the seeds. The Holy Spirit will choose the day and time to bring these seeds to fruitfulness.

But you may wonder why? Why has God declared homosexuality sinful? Does God want to deny a person sexual pleasure or a loving relationship? No! But He knows that homosexuality is not part of His design or purpose for the overcomer's eternal fulfillment or earthly happiness. Homosexuality interferes with God's loving plan for him. And what is the plan?

> For those God foreknew He also predestined to be conformed to the likeness of His Son, that He might be the firstborn among many brothers. And those He predestined, He also called; those He called, He also justified; those He justified, He also glorified (Rom. 8:29-30, KJV).

His plan is that the overcomer would be conformed to the likeness of His Son, and in Jesus is abundant life. "I have come that they may have life, and have it to the full" (John 10:10). The plan for the fullness of life began at the creation of time when God made man for woman and woman for man. The fulfillment of this plan brings glory to God. But,

> They became fools and exchanged the glory of the immortal God for idols . . . and the men abandoned natural relations with women and were inflamed with lust for one another (see Rom. 1:22, 27).

Look at this passage carefully. It declares that homosexual behavior, like other sins, arises from the refusal to honor and acknowledge God. If God is not acknowledged, if His Word is ignored, then the carnal nature will deviate from the natural heterosexual design that God intended for a man and a woman. Because of this, the person who has a tendency toward homosexuality will develop a darkened heart and a futile or foolish mind. He exchanges the glory of the immortal God for the worship of inanimate and human idols. As a result, God gives him over to the sinful desires of his heart. He then will justify abandoning natural relations with the opposite sex and will become inflamed with lust for the same sex.

If, instead, the person who has developed the psychological emotional disorientation to homosexuality would honor and acknowledge God's judgment about homosexuality, he would receive the strength and power to overcome it by the healing work of the Holy Spirit within him.

The Christian overcomer, as a saved person, therefore knows that he must change. He knows that God desires him to change because he trusts God's loving wisdom and honors Him by his belief in God's power to deliver him from the homosexual disorientation. And he can count on it!

QUESTION TWO: DO YOU WANT TO CHANGE?

When you ask your overcomer this second important question, he may say, "Of course I want to change." Yet you should still ask him to look at his desire to change more closely. What is the strength of this desire to change? What is the nature of this desire to change? He may want to change because:

— He is ashamed of the way he is living.
— He doesn't like hiding and leading a double life.
— She wants to get married and have children.
— He is afraid of exposure, of being caught.
— He doesn't like deceiving others.
— She feels that being gay doesn't fit with her self-image.
— He is afraid of getting AIDS.
— He knows that gay relationships are not permanent.
— He feels like a hypocrite as a Christian.
— He considers his lifestyle to be sinful.

These are all good reasons for desiring change. But a "desire" is not enough. Does your overcomer have only a "desire," or has he or she made a "decision" to change? A desire is a feeling; it is emotional; it is fleeting; it changes from day to day. A "decision" is a determination, a commitment, an act of one's will, motivated by a loving obedience to God and trust in the promises He has spoken to your overcomer personally through His Word. They stand up regardless of how he may feel today or tomorrow. Has he made a "decision" to be an overcomer? Does he or she have a commitment made on the hard rock of faith in God's Word? I can tell you that that's the only strength which will sustain them when they face the world's gay rhetoric, the devil's discouraging and permissive whisperings, and the weakness of their own lustful flesh. Help your overcomer to ask God to lead him or her to a verse of Scripture on which God gives a promise; on which he or she can base his or her decision to change. Suggest that they memorize such passages as,

> Commit thy way unto the Lord, trust also in Him,
> and He shall bring it to pass (Ps. 37:5, KJV).

and, that verse of Scripture which has been the miracle verse for my life and work and ministry; a verse which God has given to me personally; a verse which I have never, ever seen fail:

> In all things God works for the good of those who
> love Him, who have been called according to His
> purpose (Rom. 8:28).

and,

> Ask and it will be given to you; seek and you will
> find; knock and the door will be opened to you. For
> everyone who asks receives; he who seeks finds;
> and to him who knocks, the door will be opened
> (Matt. 7:7-8).

and,

> I will go before you and level the mountains, I will
> break down gates of bronze and cut through bars of
> iron. I will give you the treasures of darkness, rich-

es stored in secret places, so that you may know
that I am Lord, the God of Israel, who calls you by
name (Isa. 45:2-3).

Has your overcomer made a decision to change based on
these words of God? Only God's Word will sustain him during
the trials ahead in his recovery from homosexuality.

You may want to inspire him by sharing a passage of Scripture with him. You might say something like this: "Do you
hear these words of Isaiah? Do you really believe them and
trust them? Listen! He says, **'I will go before you.'** There
are a lot of obstacles in your way as you go on this journey of
healing and recovery. Frankly, I don't think you can antici-
pate what's ahead of you. But you are not the one leading the
way on this journey. He, your Lord and God, has called you
to this, and it is He who is taking the lead before you. He is
in the front line of attack. He will take the first barrage. He is
the One who is going to get wounded (He already has), and
die (He already did), so that you don't have to. Are you
listening to these precious words from God to you?

"He is telling you that He will 'level the mountains, break
down the gates of bronze' and 'cut through the bars of iron.'
He doesn't go alongside of you or behind you, but in front of
you, so that He can level the mountains, or, as the KJV says,
'make the crooked places straight.'

"There are crooked places in your heart and life which God
will straighten out as you go. He doesn't tell you that everything will be easy on this journey, but that as you get to your
seemingly insurmountable mountains, He will be there before you to level them so the climb doesn't exhaust you.
When you come to those large heavy bronze doors that you
can't open, the doors to your wounded and painful emotions,
He'll be there to help you break them down. He will also cut
through the iron bars of your defenses so that you don't have
to go on living so guarded a life as you have these many
years.

"What will He give you as you begin this journey and start
to progress? He will give you 'the treasures of darkness, the
riches stored in secret places.' What He will give you is the
freedom to experience your emotional and spiritual life deep-

ly and abundantly, something you have not really experienced all your life.

"Deep inside you where your inner child was hurt and wounded, you have been emotionally restricted and limited. But you will recover these secret treasures and experience a new emotional and spiritual depth and freedom like you have never known before. This is the healing I have witnessed when the Holy Spirit works through the counselors whom He has called to help you in this work of healing and recovery.

" 'So that you may know that I am the Lord, the God of Israel.' This journey through the healing of homosexuality is going to do even more than help you recover your heterosexuality. You are going to really come to know the Lord God, and worship and enjoy Him forever. Praise God!

"God says to you that He has called you to this journey 'by name.' Do you hear what He is saying? He has called you by name. He knows you by name; you, individually. He has been listening to the desire of your heart to be healed of homosexuality. He has heard you; you as an individual. He knows all about you as a unique individual. He knows your own beginning from your mother's womb (Ps. 139). He knows all about how homosexuality got started in you, and He knows how to heal it, with your cooperation. He knows you; He knows you by name, and by name He has called you to this journey of healing. Amen! and Amen!

"Don't leave these words of God until they form the rock foundation of your decision to want to change. STOP! Make that decision right now! Don't go any further until you do! You see, **Fact number two** is **you want to change, and have decided to change based on the trustworthiness of the Word of God.** You have made a Bible-based, God-promised commitment and determination to change."

QUESTION THREE: DO YOU KNOW THAT YOU REALLY CAN CHANGE?
Fact number three: homosexuality can be overcome. The person you are counseling can overcome homosexuality and can even recover his or her heterosexuality. Literally thousands have done this and are doing this. People have not only left the lifestyle, not only stopped the sinful homosexual

behavior, but they have recovered heterosexual desires. Heterosexual feelings and desires do return. Marriages can be strengthened and renewed. Homosexual attractions do decline and diminish. The big "H" of homosexuality becomes a small "h." There is HOPE!

However, let us not overstate this good news about recovery from homosexuality. While you want your overcomer to maintain enthusiasm about the change which the Lord will work in him or her, at the same time you want to be realistic. What do I mean by recovery? What is a realistic expectation? What is recovery? Here is a carefully worded definition based upon my experience in ministry thus far.

> Recovery is being able to go on with your personal and relational life goals and plans with minimally bothersome homosexual feelings, thoughts, desires, and attractions (temptations), and avoiding all homosexual behavior, (1) by knowing what you are experiencing physically and emotionally, and (2) by choosing what to do and what not to do; based on a foundation of personality renewal and healing through the sustaining power of the Holy Spirit.

Please note some important things in this definition. First, recovery includes the ability to go on with career, educational, family, and marital plans. For recovery to be effective at all, homosexuality should not stand in the way of life goals and plans. A recovering overcomer should experience enough freedom to pursue his life goals productively instead of feeling hampered, restricted, inhibited, and limited. Jesus brings a full life and a fulfilling life.

This is an important aspect of recovery because achieving life goals and plans is closely tied in with ending the homosexual disorientation. They must go together. A person's self-image and self-esteem is largely based on what he thinks and feels about himself. Improved self-image and self-esteem are dependent upon achieving these life goals and plans. Poor self-image (PSI) and low self-esteem (LSE) are at the root of the homosexual disorientation. As we will see later, poor self-image and low self-esteem form the initial emotional deficits which are foundational causes of the homosexual disorientation.

Second, the recovering overcomer is going to come to a time when he will have such freedom and emotional strength through the power of Christ's Spirit in him, that homosexual behavior will have ceased altogether, and such feelings, thoughts, desires, and attractions will be only minimally troublesome. He will be able to manage these without great inner conflict, tension, or turmoil.

One overcomer described the change in this analogy.

> Once I had a painful sliver in my finger which caused my finger to be infected, swollen and very sore. I was able to take most of the sliver out by my own efforts, at least the part that was visible and that I could get a hold of. But some of it remained, causing the finger to remain infected and sensitive for a time. I knew that the sliver would eventually work its way out through the body's natural healing process. I knew that the swelling would eventually go down and that the soreness would stop after awhile. All I could do was to keep it clean, bathe it regularly, medicate it as best as I could, and avoid hitting it until it healed.
>
> Once in awhile, during that time of healing, I accidentally hit it and felt some real pain. But most of the time I didn't notice the pain at all and forgot all about having the sliver. Then it eventually healed itself completely. Throughout most of this whole time, I went on with my work and life forgetting all about the soreness I felt in my finger.

You see, recovery doesn't mean your overcomer will never notice an attractive same-sex person again or that he will never be tempted again. It does mean that he will be in control and that homosexuality will not control his life. It does mean that homosexuality can and will fade into the untroublesome background of his life.

Third, recovery means the ability to manage such temptations because he has learned enough about himself to recognize what is really going on with him physically, emotionally, and spiritually. For instance, he has learned physical triggers that arise when he is physically ill, tired, tense, stressed, and pressured. He has learned about his emotional triggers; those times when his sensitive inner child is feeling frightened, angry, sad, humiliated, victimized, lonely, empty, overwhelmed, and sorry for himself. He will have come to learn how to name his feelings, really feel and face them, talk to himself about them realistically and honestly, and act appropriately on them (proact).

He will have learned how to recognize and manage these wounded emotions. He will have learned that he engages in transferences with people who affect him like his own parents affected him, and how this stimulates his critical inner parent. He will have learned to make proactive choices; choices that are positive and constructive.

Last, notice that recovery is based on a foundation of general personality renewal and healing. Much of what heals homosexuality from a psychological perspective is the renewal of a person's emotional thinking and acting patterns. These changes cause overcomers to experience greater emotional growth, stability, self-control, joy, peace, patience, selflessness, contentment, less stress and tension, and greater spiritual maturity. This good fruit is a result of the sustaining activity and the healing power of the Holy Spirit; the Spirit of Christ in your overcomer.

Fact number four: It is the willful indulgence in homosexual behavior (thoughts and actions) which is sinful, not the disorientation. Only that which is willfully indulged in can be considered sin. All the rest is temptation. The overcomer must learn to make this distinction. Many are intolerant of even the slightest temptation. They feel that even having temptation is sinful. Instead, they should only consider what they foster and indulge in to be sinful. Feelings, attractions, urges, desires, longings, are all temptations. Acting on any of these mentally or physically is sin.

Fact number five: Homosexuality is learned. God made no one homosexual; nor did one's genes, hormones, or biology. God makes everyone heterosexual. I do recognize certain factors which may predispose someone to emotional disorder such as birth defects and pre-birth sensitivities, though none of these cause homosexuality. Therefore, over-comers are heterosexual people with a homosexual disorien-tation which is learned. Kronemeyer says,

> With rare exceptions, homosexuality is neither in-herited nor the result of some glandular distur-bance or the scrambling of genes or chromosomes. Homosexuals are made, not born that way. From my 25 years experience as a clinical psychologist, I firmly believe that homosexuality is a learned re-sponse to early painful experiences and that it can be unlearned.[1]

My own experience confirms this very thing. Homosexual-ity is a disorientation which is psychologically, emotionally learned. I have seen many people change this disorientation as they begin to relearn to experience their emotional self in more positive ways. The homosexual behavior results from this emotional disorientation as external manifestations and symptoms.

Fact number six: No one chooses to be or feel homo-sexual initially. It was not a choice your overcomer made early in life when it began as an emotional disorientation. It happened to him at a very early stage of life. It arose from the early environmental experiences which he had with his par-ents, peers and siblings, and other significant people such as teachers and pastors. It especially has to do with the dissatis-fying love bond which he had with his mother and father, but most often with the parent of the same gender.

Later in life homosexuality became temptation, same sex attraction, and a sinful behavioral choice which he willfully made when he indulged homosexual feelings, thoughts, and attractions.

Fact number seven: Homosexuality has very little to do with sex. It has much more to do with an emotional and psychological wound which leaves a person feeling deprived, empty, unfulfilled, and incomplete in the bonding that he needed to experience with the same gender parent. Further-more, he feels overwhelmed, victimized, and short on self-esteem. The sexual aspect of homosexuality is an attempt to meet the love and intimacy needs which were never adequately formed between the child and the same-sex parent. As such, it is really not a sexual problem at all. It is only sexual in how it relates to the intimacy needs that sexuality symbolizes.

Dr. Elizabeth Moberly, who has done extensive research on the development of homosexuality, speaks of the "reparative urge that is involved in the homosexual impulse." The impulse "is essentially motivated by the need to make good earlier deficits in the parent-child relationship. The persisting need for love from the same sex stems from . . . the earlier unmet need for love from the parent of the same sex, or rather, the inability to receive such love, whether or not it was offered."[2]

QUESTION FOUR:
DO YOU KNOW HOW TO CHANGE?

Fact number eight: homosexuality is an emotional, psychological, spiritual problem. It is neither only spiritual or psychological. People who propose that it is exclusively either one or the other do a disservice to overcomers.

The proponents of exclusive psychological remedies ignore the reality that homosexual behavior is rooted in our sin nature inherited from Adam. They also ignore the essential work of the Holy Spirit in the healing of homosexuality and in the wider purposes God is effecting in the person's life. The proponents of exclusive spiritual healing approaches ignore the emotional causes and roots of homosexuality and the practical human realities of psychological change.

Fact number nine: Recovery is a process that takes time. The most frequent prayer of overcomers goes something like this:

"Lord, deliver me from all homosexuality right now, instantly and completely." Then because they are not instantly and completely healed, they become discouraged, angry at God, and their faith begins to evaporate.

Why doesn't God instantly and completely heal homosexuality as a result of this sincere prayer? Some say that when they were saved they felt completely free from homosexuality for a period of months and even years; but most report the return of homosexual attractions, feelings, and desires, or even find themselves having a "fall" (a sexual encounter). Why is it that God heals through a process that takes time? I believe that in His loving wisdom, there are at least six reasons why God progressively heals a person of homosexuality over time; a healing which I have described in my definition of recovery.

1. **God never violates free will.** The fact is, God knows that the overcomer has moments when he or she really and sincerely wants to be free from homosexuality; but He also knows that there are times when he or she freely chooses to sin in this way. God knows us even better than we know ourselves. He knows the real person. He knows the heart. Over a period of time He will cause him or her to freely and willingly choose His will over his or her own. He desires them to come into a heart-to-heart relationship with Him. He intends to draw them into loving obedience to His will. He desires to teach them in a gradual way that His will is really best. This has always been God's way with us. He seeks complete and freely chosen obedience in the healing of homosexuality.

2. **He desires that your overcomer use human effort and strength in conjunction with the working of the Holy Spirit.** This arises from the Lord's love for your overcomer. He desires to have your overcomer experience God's power working within him. God does not want to simply change the overcomer. He wants your overcomer to exert his own will and effort. For God to bypass your overcomer's cooperation in the healing process would be a violation of the way that God designed him as a human-spiritual being. He would deny him the experience of personal victory in himself. God expects him to will and want and do his part. Augustine said it so well, "Without God, man cannot; without man, God will not."

3. **God does not violate the integrity of your personality.** It took time to develop the homosexual complex over a period of years which made homosexuality an integrated part of the fabric of your personality. It is woven into your self-image and self-esteem. Therefore, in the usual course of

things, it takes time to unweave and reweave your personality.

4. God is in the process of renewing your whole personality. He cannot and will not remove the homosexual elements in you, which are, after all, merely manifestations and symptoms (not an alternative sexuality or lifestyle as gays might say), without the renewal of the whole person and the very roots of homosexuality.

5. God desires to renew you spiritually. As He works with your freely given cooperation, honoring the integrity of your personality, He will draw you into a deeper heart-to-heart relationship with Himself as you continually turn to Him in faith, in hope, and in love.

6. God watches over your psychological-emotional stability. Consider the paradox involved in God instantly changing you this very moment. Such an abrupt change would leave you disarmed, perplexed, and psychologically in crisis. It would be like changing you from a cat to a canary. You would still be alive but you would have no idea who you were or how to function. Think about it! This is not God's way.

Fact number ten: Homosexuality is not only your private trouble; it is a public issue. You need to see your private trouble with homosexuality in a larger perspective. Homosexuality is a disorientation which comes out of dysfunctional family environments. Like the alarmingly increasing rates of suicides, missing and runaway children, abortions, divorces, child pornography, rapes, physical and sexual abuse of children, drug abuse and alcoholism, homosexuality is one of the many outward symptoms of the dysfunctional family.

The increasing number of dysfunctional families, in turn, arises from the pervasive and profound loss of biblical values and standards in our whole society. Furthermore, there is a godlessness that we see through all social institutions. Homosexual behavior and the homosexual disorientation results from this public and societal godlessness. The gay liberation rhetoric is reflective of this general moral decay which has even infiltrated our traditional denominational churches and theology.

FOR THE COUNSELOR

In my counseling work with overcomers I quickly became aware of the importance of building a committed relationship. Since overcoming homosexuality has so many ups and downs, your overcomer will need to experience you as a person whom he can trust and turn to when he has doubts and discouragements. You will need a good deal of patience and steadfastness. You will need to be for him a godly example. Your faithfulness, caring, patience, ability to be nonjudgmental, and endurance will be for him God's love made tangible.

Therefore, it is most important that you settle these four questions and ten facts for yourself in a genuine way. You cannot work effectively with overcomers if you have a double-mindedness about these issues yourself. If you remain confused, it will be difficult for you to be convincing about your commitment to help him overcome homosexuality and move on to a more God-pleasing lifestyle.

Do you really understand why the Lord views homosexuality as sin? Do you know in your heart that it is God's love that calls the homosexual sinner to change? Do you really believe that healing is possible? Have you settled the issue of what is expectable in terms of healing? What are you implicitly promising your overcomer? Is the definition of recovery too broad; too narrow; too ideal; too limited for you?

Does your overcomer have solid reasons for desiring change? Have you emphasized the importance of the need for him to seek the Lord's Word for a verse or passage on which he can base his "decision" to change? He will need a firm faith in God's Word, not just in you, when he is severely tempted, when he is discouraged, when he backslides, when he slips or has a fall.

Begin to help your overcomer change his language and thinking. Help him distinguish between temptation and sin, between the spiritual and emotional, between the satanic and the psychological, between symptoms and root causes, between acceptance of himself as a person struggling with homosexuality and acceptance of homosexuality. Help him love himself as a sinner, though he despises his sin. Lastly, help him to discontinue calling himself gay or homosexual, which is labeling himself with an unchangeable identity. Instead, remind him that God made him a heterosexual person, though he has a homosexual struggle. Have him call himself an "overcomer."

1. Robert Kronemeyer, *Overcoming Homosexuality* (New York: Macmillan, 1980), 7.
2. Elizabeth R. Moberly, *Homosexuality: A New Christian Ethic* (Cambridge, England: James Clarke, 1983), 11.

CHAPTER THREE

ALL THINGS WORK TOGETHER FOR GOOD: SPIRITUAL RENEWAL

The healing of homosexuality involves two things. Your overcomer must make positive changes in his external behavior and environment. Under the power of the Spirit, there needs to be healing change within his personality. The framework for helping your overcomer is divided into external and internal changes. There must be behavioral changes and inner healing. While both kinds of change require his own efforts, they especially require the transforming power of the Holy Spirit in his heart. Remember, homosexuality is both a psychological and a spiritual problem. While God did not give your overcomer the homosexual problem, He fully intends to use His healing as a means of accomplishing His loving purposes for his whole life. He fully intends to make all things work together for His good because he loves God and has been called by God according to His purposes (Rom. 8:28).

As you begin this journey with your overcomer, he must be sure that his Guide and Counselor is the Holy Spirit. God purposes to heal homosexuality in him through His Holy Spirit as he works in his changed heart-to-heart relationship with the Lord; as the overcomer is continually sanctified and made holy by the challenges of faith, hope, and love of God presented to him, and as he chooses to serve God and others from the heart-to-heart relationship he has with the Lord. It is important to help your overcomer become grounded in this real relationship with the Lord.

As you begin this healing work with your overcomer, you will need to remind him over and over again that the healing of homosexuality is not his first priority. Instead, he must make his relationship with God his first priority, knowing that "all things will work together for good" if the love of God is his first priority.

He is God's first priority. His whole, renewed, and sanctified body, soul, and human spirit is the Lord's first priority. The Lord seeks his heart, his commitment, his love, and his trust in Him. He seeks a real relationship with him.

> Seek first His kingdom and His righteousness, and all these things will be given to you as well. Therefore, do not worry about tomorrow (Matt. 6:33-34).

Say to your overcomer, "Do not worry about your homosexuality. Take your eyes off of your homosexuality. Homosexuality will be, hear me, will be healed in His time and in His way as He begins to accomplish the three loving purposes He has for you because He loves you." What are those three purposes? He desires your overcomer to be saved, sanctified, and active in serving Him and others — salvation, sanctification, and service. Salvation results from the changes which He effects in his heart. Sanctification comes from the spiritual challenges which will be placed on his life and heart as He heals him. Service results from the choices which your overcomer must make from his heart; increasingly, gratefully, and freely. All of these form the heart-to-heart relationship with God which He desires to have with your overcomer.

CHANGES OF THE HEART

Tell your overcomer, "God wants you to have a new and changed heart. It is your deepest spiritual heart that He is most interested in. He desires worshipers who worship Him from their deepest transformed and committed hearts. Salvation means having a new and renewed heart. Salvation brings the experience of a changed heart and brings you into a relationship with God which is one "in spirit and in truth" (John 4:23). And so, the first question to ask is: "Are you a saved person?" Has he made Jesus Christ his own and personal Savior, Lord, and Master? Has he come into a personal relationship to the Father through the Holy Spirit's work and his acceptance of Christ as his Savior in faith?

> Jesus answered, "I am the way, the truth, and the life. No one comes to the Father except through Me" (John 14:6).

and,

> No one has ever seen God, but God the only Son, who is at the Father's side, has made Him known (John 1:18).

Before you go any farther in this journey of healing with your overcomer, be sure he is a saved person. What does he have to do to become a saved person? He must believe the Gospel message that Christ died for our sins according to the Scripture, that He was buried, that He was raised on the third day according to the Scriptures (1 Cor. 15:3-4).

Christ died for his sins as the Scriptures foretold that He would in the Old Testament prophecies, and as the New Testament Scriptures verified that He did. Christ was his personal sinbearer. Christ who knew no sin took upon Himself the penalty and the punishment that we deserve as members of a sinful humanity and for our own personal sins. He took our place so that we could regain a right standing (righteousness) with God.

To receive this free gift of salvation from God only requires that the overcomer accept what Jesus accomplished for him in faith, and acknowledge Jesus as his Savior who restored him to relationship with God the Father. John says, "To all who received Him, to those who believed in His name, He gave the right to become children of God" (John 1:12). John also says, "God so loved the world that He gave His only begotten Son, that whosoever believes in Him shall not perish but have eternal life" (John 3:16, NASB). And in Romans it says, "Everyone who calls on the name of the Lord will be saved" (Rom. 10:13).

If your overcomer has never prayed for salvation, or if he

needs to renew his prayer of salvation as he begins this work of healing, do that first. Have him say these words sincerely and honestly.

> Lord Jesus! I believe that You are the only Son of God who came among us so that I might be saved and come to know the Father through a changed heart-to-heart relationship with Him. I believe that You died for my sins, that You rose from the dead, and that You will send me Your Holy Spirit. Jesus, I truly desire to accept what You did for me and I thank You for loving me. I want You to be my Lord and Savior and I know that You will heal me of this burden of homosexuality in Your own time and way. Thank You, Jesus! Amen!

SIGNS OF A NEW HEART

A person who is saved has a new, spiritually alive heart. The Holy Spirit has quickened (given spiritual life to) your overcomer's human spirit or heart. He now has God's own Spirit-filled life in him.

What are some of the results of this changed and renewed heart? Here are twelve of them. Depending on how long he has been saved and the development of his spiritual maturity, he will see these signs in differing degrees. Let me put this in the first person singular, as if I were talking directly to an overcomer.

1. You will pray sincerely and eagerly from the heart. This will be done honestly, willingly, and spontaneously.

2. You will frequently want to praise God and thank Him for His many blessings in your life.

3. You will be interested in searching and understanding the Bible because you now realize that it is God's Word. You will find that He speaks to you personally from His written Word.

4. You will want to share your faith with others and will want to be with others who share your faith.

5. Your attitudes, values, and desires will increasingly be more godly even though you will continue to struggle with the big "H" for a time.

6. You will seek after holiness and goodness and will begin to dislike sin in all its forms. Homosexual sins will never again be engaged in without some conflict and remorse.

7. You will also begin to feel more self-accepting and properly self-loving. You will also be more tolerant, kind, and loving toward others, but also more eager to see others change their sinful habits.

8. You will sense the Holy Spirit dwelling and acting more powerfully in your heart and life.

9. You will begin to want to know God more intimately and will lovingly and meaningfully begin to call Him Father.

10. You will want to serve God in some way.

11. You will be more aware of sin and Satan in the world and seek to discern good from evil more effectively.

12. You will experience more power; power over sin and Satan.

THE UNCONSCIOUS BURIAL GROUND

The heart of a person is the human spirit. It is the deepest dimension of his personality which in psychology is referred to as the unconscious (see diagram #1, p. 103). In the heart is the "burial ground" of painful forgotten events, emotions, hurts, wounds, fixed ideas and impressions, troubling anxieties, fears, defenses, and sins from the past. This unconscious buried past continues to influence his whole personality and behavior in negative ways. Later, we will see that the work done on these wounded emotions, fixed impressions, and guarded defenses is the critical internal change which heals homosexuality from within and renews his whole personality. Jesus said,

> What comes out of a man is what makes him "unclean." For from within, out of men's hearts come evil thoughts, sexual immorality, theft, murder, adultery, greed, malice, deceit, lewdness, envy, slander, arrogance, and folly. All these evils come from inside (Mark 7:20-23).

God's Word also says, "Above all else, guard your heart, for it is the wellspring of life" (Prov. 4:23). As the KJV says,

"Keep thy heart with all diligence; for out of it are the issues of life."

The heart is by nature hard. It is compared to a stone that feels nothing. It has no feeling or sensitivity for spiritual things. It is unrepentant and stubborn (Rom. 2:5) and it is deceitful (Jer. 17:9). This is why we need a new and renewed heart. This is why we need to be saved by the Word and the Holy Spirit.

THE DWELLING PLACE OF THE HOLY SPIRIT

When the Holy Spirit enters the heart or human spirit at the time of salvation, He makes the hard heart softer; the proud heart humble; the worldly heart more spiritual.

> I will give you a new heart and put a new spirit within you; I will remove from you your heart of stone and give you a heart of flesh. And I will put My Spirit in you (Ezek. 36:26-27).

and so,

> Rid yourself of all offenses you have committed, and get a new heart and a new spirit (Ezek. 18:31).

Therefore,

> If you confess with your mouth, "Jesus is Lord," and believe in your heart that God raised Him from the dead, you will be saved. For it is from your heart that you believe and are justified (Rom. 10:9).

A person comes into a whole new relationship with God when he is saved or quickened by the Holy Spirit, for, "The Spirit gives life; the flesh counts for nothing" (John 6:63). Romans says, "If anyone does not have the spirit of Christ, he does not belong to Christ" (Rom. 8:9). As a saved person your overcomer has turned him or herself over to God.

> Your body is a temple of the Holy Spirit, who is in you, whom you have received from God. You are

not your own, you were bought with a price. Therefore, honor God with your body (1 Cor. 6:19-20).

This is the heart change which also is the foundation for healing homosexuality through the presence and the power of the Holy Spirit who dwells within.

CHALLENGES OF THE HEART
Through the changed heart of salvation God has brought your overcomer into a spiritual relationship with Himself; a heart-to-heart relationship. Now He purposes to develop what was born anew in him or her. He purposes to make the person sanctified, holy, and set apart for Himself. As he daily lives by faith, by hope, and by his love of God, he will be challenged to continually be, "controlled not by the sinful nature but by the Spirit, if the Spirit of God lives in [him]" (Rom. 8:9).

God purposes to make your overcomer holy through the renewing of his old sinful nature and to make him more and more conformed into the likeness of Christ (Col. 2:10). God is all holiness; and the Scriptures say, "Holy, holy, holy is the Lord Almighty" (Isa. 6:3).

He purposes to heal his homosexuality by drawing him toward the fire of His holiness. There, before His great holiness, your overcomer will feel the cleansing heat from his closeness to the Lord.

> Therefore, prepare your minds for action; be self-controlled; set your hope fully on the grace to be given you when Jesus Christ is revealed. As obedient children, do not conform to the evil desires you had when you lived in ignorance. But just as he who called you is holy, so be holy in all you do; for it is written: "Be holy, because I am holy" (1 Peter 1:13-16).

He will be challenged to live by God's high standard of holiness so that he will become more and more holy himself. These challenges will act as disciplines to the old carnal nature that keeps homosexuality alive. These challenges of the heart will be painful and trying to him, "but God disciplines us for our own good, that we may share in His holiness" (Heb. 12:10). As there can be no communion between dark and light, there can be no communion between the holy God and an unholy sinner. For "without holiness no one will see the Lord" (Heb. 12:14). God who made man for communion with Himself, purposes to restore holiness to you, for only the pure in heart shall see God (Matt. 5:8).

Say to your overcomer that by the blood of Christ the guilt of your sin is taken from you. By the Spirit of Christ you were born again and made into a new creature fit to be restored for the communion with God in heaven where, "we shall see face to face. Now I know in part; then I shall know fully, even as I am fully known" (1 Cor. 13:12).

THE CHALLENGE OF FAITH
One of the challenges your overcomer will confront is the challenge of faith. Faith is the spiritual movement of his heart which connects him with God who is Spirit. Those who have been saved shall live by faith (Rom. 1:17). He will continually have to walk by the dim light of faith in the healing of homosexuality. He will not have a floodlight of sight to see the day-to-day incremental changes of homosexual healing. He will have many a day when he will wonder whether anything is changing at all. He will have to continually reach out to God in faith which is the evidence for things that are unseen (Heb. 11:1). Homosexual healing is an internal change which is spiritual, emotional, and subtle.

THE CHALLENGE OF HOPE
On this journey of healing and growth in holiness, your overcomer needs assistance to maintain his hope. He will absolutely need hope. The Bible says, "We have this hope as an anchor for the soul, firm and secure" (Heb. 6:19).

Say to your overcomer, "Hope is an anchor when this journey gets rough like a small boat at sea. You will need the anchor of hope when you feel lost and off course. Your heart needs hope or you will get sick at heart (Prov. 13:12) and will even lose the desire to pursue this journey of healing. Hope enables you to reach beyond your present experience and to take hold of the goal which you have set for yourself even when it is very elusive. And where does hope come from? It comes from the very sufferings and discouragements which this journey presents to you."

> We also rejoice in our sufferings, because we know that suffering produces perseverance; perseverance character; and character hope. And hope does not disappoint us (Rom. 5:3-5).

This is one of the aspects of the healing of homosexuality. The more one perseveres in suffering and temptation, the more he develops strength of character. This self-awareness of growing inner strength produces more and more hope. In turn, this allows him to persevere in suffering and develop more character strength.

It is just this kind of inner strength that heals the emotional wounded area within him and eliminates the need for him to look to other same-gender persons for self-acceptance and approval.

THE CHALLENGE OF LOVE

Love is the biggest spiritual challenge of all. Love is a challenge not only to his relationship to God but with others as well. The lack of love, or that poorly developed love-bond in childhood, is at the root of the homosexual problem. It is love, when absent, inadequate, or distorted, which forms the first problems with self-esteem and gender emptiness.

Love is what your overcomer needed most and needs most. Love is often what the overcomer has the most difficulty giving and receiving. Love, in its many forms – approval, acceptance, being valued, worthwhile, cherished, being special and important – is the basic thing which went wrong in early childhood for overcomers. It is the thing that most attracts them to people of the same gender long before it ever becomes sexualized and eroticized. Love, praise God, is also the most healing and renewing force in the world. Your love for your overcomer; your mature and generous love, will provide the healing relationship which supports the journey to recovery.

HOW LOVE HEALS

Why is love such a powerful force for healing? Fundamentally because love is the most basic similarity we all share with our Creator God, who is our Father and who is LOVE. Because God is love, He is all truth, all wholeness, all goodness, all peace, all fullness, all life. Love is the central characteristic of the human race as God created us in His own image.

Love is also the lifeline between human beings. It is the deepest experience of contact and communion which two people can have with each other. It is most satisfying. It is most fulfilling. Love is therefore always at the heart of the healing of homosexuality. Your overcomer will need large injections of love from you and his Christian brothers and sisters. Help your overcomer to begin to open herself or himself to love. Be sure that you yourself are a person who feels loved and is able to be maturely loving with others. Be sure that you have the capacity to be unconditionally loving with others.

CHOICES OF THE HEART

Your overcomer has experienced a change of heart if he has truly been born again and saved. He will be continually disciplined by the challenges he faces as he exercises his faith, hope, and love. Because of his growing faith, hope, and love he will increasingly want to choose or make choices from a loving and grateful heart which please God and help him to walk in that heart-to-heart relationship with the Lord.

It is important for you, the counselor, to help him to regularly engage in five essential spirit-sustaining and life-sustaining choices.

1. **Prayer and worship** is essential to maintaining his heart-to-heart relationship with God and the inner healing which God desires to do within him. He must get serious about prayer and worship because God deserves his worship and because he needs to pray. God does not need his worship and prayer, but God does deserve it. A willing and loving heart cannot help but give God what He is worthy of.

Explain to your overcomer that prayer and worship is the spiritual (Spirit-led) language of his heart and God's heart. It is his way to speak of his gratefulness, his love, his obedience, adoration, and praise. It is also a time to tell God about his guilt and shame, his remorse and pain, his repentance from sin, his needs and wants, and his longing and desire to be healed. He must bring everything to God in prayer. God is our Father who hears our secret prayers when we go into the closet of solitude and communion with the Lord. He has said, "Therefore I tell you, whatever you ask in prayer, believe that you have received it, and it will be yours" (Mark 11:24).

2. **Daily conversation with the Lord** is a good practice for the overcomer. This means that he should get into the habit of speaking to the Lord or meditating on the Lord frequently and regularly during the day. Keeping up a dialogue with the Lord during the day is a way of being in His presence continually. Speak to Him truthfully, lovingly, and openly about the day's trials and hassles, joys and satisfactions. He can say simple things like: "Thank You, Lord; help me, Lord; what do You want me to do, Lord? How do I solve this, Lord? or I love You, Father; I love You, Jesus; I love You, Holy Spirit." He can also quote favorite Bible verses which have special meaning for him.

If he makes these daily conversations a regular practice, he will see the number of times during the day when he senses being directed and guided by the Lord. He will see himself gaining greater control over his temptations and sexual distractions.

> The eyes of all wait upon Thee; and Thou givest
> them their meat in due season (Ps. 145:15, KJV),

and,

> But by faith we eagerly await through the Spirit the
> righteousness for which we hope (Gal. 5:5).

Later we will look at the great importance which you, the counselor, must place on the way in which your overcomer engages in conversation with the Lord. We will see that many times these conversations are distorted and inaccurate, often the result of the human "father filter" through which the overcomer views his relationship with God.

3. **Regular Bible study and meditation** is another choice which flows from the overcomer's changed and sancti-

fied heart. The overcomer must make continuous contact with God's chosen method for speaking and motivating His children: His Word, the Bible.

How can God speak to the one struggling with homosexuality if he is not listening? How can the Lord feed His children if the overcomer is not coming to the table to be fed? How will the Lord guide your overcomer and direct his paths unless he is willing to come to the light of His Word? The Bible says, "The unfolding of Your words gives light, it gives understanding to the simple" (Ps. 119:130).

May I especially suggest the following passages which I have found speak strongly to those who seek healing: The Letter to the Ephesians; the Letter of James; Luke 10:21-28, 30-37; Colossians 3:1-17; 2 Corinthians 4:1-15.

4. **Christian fellowship** in a good Bible teaching and preaching church is most important. Here the overcomer will be able to build good Christian male and female relationships. He will have the support of the body of Christ, a supportive pastor and elders, and an opportunity to grow in the family of Christ. The overcomer should not be kept apart from the congregation because he struggles with homosexuality. He needs just the opposite—equal and full participation and responsibility in his church. If his problem with homosexuality may have effects on those he works with in church ministry or cause difficulties there, the pastor/counselor must use his good judgment and discernment in the roles the overcomer may assume.

Also, the overcomer should not be made to prematurely give his testimony in the church congregation. This could cause the kind of vulnerability which may be destructive to his spiritual and emotional growth. Rather, it is better if he shares his struggle with selected, trustworthy church members who will respect confidentiality.

5. **A special friend.** This is a trustworthy person who is a Christian and with whom the overcomer can be accountable and share his struggles regularly. It should not be a person who has had or has this same problem, yet it must be a person with whom the overcomer can be frank and open. If your overcomer sincerely desires to overcome homosexuality, he must begin to share this burden with someone who

will accept him and listen to him with compassion and care. He needs this "straight" person who is not his counselor or pastor.

FOR THE COUNSELOR

The healing of homosexuality has to do with both external and internal changes. These changes require the overcomer's own efforts but he must also harness the power of the Holy Spirit who is the real Healer, the real Counselor, the real Guide and Comforter.

The Holy Spirit comes into the overcomer's heart to make him a changed person who is spiritually alive and sensitive. He will discipline him through the challenges of faith, hope, and love which your overcomer must inevitably face. Salvation, sanctification, and service; these are the spiritual foundations which you, the helper, must initiate and reinforce with your overcomer. These are the spiritual essentials needed to make all things begin to work together for good.

There is no journey to take for your overcomer if he is not well-grounded in these essentials. He needs this heart-to-heart relationship with the Lord. Jesus said,

> I will show you what he is like who comes to Me and hears My words and puts them into practice. He is like a man building a house who dug down deep and laid the foundation on rock. When a flood came, a torrent struck that house but could not shake it (Luke 6:47-48).

The overcomer can expect to be struck by the torrents of doubt, fear, sadness, unwillingness, anger, discouragement, impatience, and temptation on this journey to heal homosexuality. Be sure you have helped him to build his house on the rock of God's Word and a real heart-to-heart relationship with Jesus.

From time to time review his spiritual life. Make periodic assessments of those challenges to his faith, his hope, and his love. Is he continuing good fellowship at his church; engaging in daily prayer and regular Bible study/meditation? What is the quality of his worship and the frequency of those daily conversations with the Lord? Does he meet with his special friend or attend his support ministry regularly?

If you have prepared him well with this spiritual foundation of strength and cleared the ground of personal motivation with those first four questions and ten facts, he is ready to find out why he didn't choose homosexuality.

I NEVER CHOSE
TO BE HOMOSEXUAL

That's right! Your overcomer never chose to feel homosexual feelings, desires, or have homosexual thoughts and attractions; at least initially. The development of homosexuality was not a conscious choice initially. We know a good deal about how it all began and the way that homosexuality develops. That is what this chapter is all about.

However, before I begin to describe the stages of homosexual development, let's take a moment to see the whole framework of reorientation therapy again and to understand where you are going and what you are working to achieve.

I would ask you to take another look at that foundation of personal motivation again. Are his answers to those four questions showing that his faith, hope, and trust in the Lord are shaky? Are the ten facts showing up again and again as issues he wants to argue or is unable to understand? Is he showing impatience with the process? Are you getting a lot of resistance?

Your overcomer, while born again, may be struggling with the challenges of faith, hope, and love. He will need continuous reinforcement in these spiritual areas of his life. There is nothing wrong with taking the time to do an inspiring Bible study with him during one of your counseling sessions. He may need this every so often. Keep tabs on all these things. They're important.

In this chapter, you will be helping your overcomer develop an understanding of how homosexuality developed in his life. This is very, very important, and an essential building block of reorientation therapy. While in the second chapter you helped him to understand homosexuality in general, and in the third chapter you focused on his spiritual walk with the Lord, in this chapter you will help him understand how homosexuality began in him specifically and how the Lord has begun to heal him.

But I don't want to make this some kind of theoretical presentation about homosexual causation and etiology. Instead, I want to make this a personal experience through which you can help your overcomer recapture his own roots of how homosexuality began in his life. I want to help you to help him or her get in touch with each stage of its development through questions, memories, and some exercises. These may be a little discomforting for the overcomer. They may unsettle and upset him. It may make him feel angry, discouraged, hopeless, and upset. But remind him that, "All things are working together for his good" (see Rom. 8:28).

First, what is homosexuality? **Homosexuality is sexual interest in, activity with, and many times, strong emotional attachment to a person of the same sex.** It primarily develops out of the early childhood experience of a poorly established love-bonding relationship with the parent of the same gender. This seems to be the most critical factor which gives rise to homosexuality.

But while it arises from that learned experience, sometimes a person may be more vulnerable to homosexuality because of pre-birth, predisposing factors. Some of these may be chromosomal complexities or a certain sensitive temperament.

Ed Hurst writes:

> If we consider any or all of the previously mentioned factors to be possible, it follows, then, that we are not simply the "product of our environment" but that we are "the product of our environment" **and** these inborn factors. This could explain why two individuals who share essentially the same environment develop different personalities.

The inborn factors cause them to react to their environment differently.

He goes on to say:

It is my belief that some "inborn" factors may contribute to the development of homosexual attractions and identity but that (1) they are not sufficient in themselves to produce homosexuality; (2) they do not always produce homosexuality; and (3) homosexual attractions and identity that are partially rooted in "inborn" causes are not irreversible.[1]

So, note well! None of these predispositions alone or together form a homosexual disorientation. What is always seen are other environmental or developmental factors such as the behavior of the other sex parent, medical handicaps or problems, the impact of the birth order, sibling sex ratios, dysfunctional family relationships, early sexual abuse or exploitation, emotional abuse and rejection, dissatisfying peer relationships.

THE CONSPIRACY THEORY

Together, all of the factors conspire to effect an emotional wounding which leaves the child with Low Self-Esteem (LSE) and Gender Emptiness (GE); a gender identity insecurity or inadequacy. It is the inner healing of that emotional woundedness which brings strength and gender wholeness to the inner man, reducing and eliminating the homosexual need and allowing heterosexual functioning to emerge.

It is this "conspiracy of factors theory" which makes the overcomer angry at God. He often feels like he unfairly has been given a homosexual "curse" by God. He often has asked despairingly and discouragingly, "Why, God? Why me?"

STAGES OF INTEGRATION

Effective and genuine healing does not take place unless the overcomer gradually moves through several stages of integration. He must move from anger/discouragement/self-rejection; to acceptance of this struggle within him; to self-acceptance of himself as a person; to integration of the homosexual struggle from seeing it as his whole identity to recognition that he is much more than "homosexual." Finally, he must arrive at an embracing of the homosexual struggle as his spiritual opportunity which makes him truly understand that "all things," even his struggle with homosexuality, "works together for good"; and that "in all these things we are more than conquerors through Him who loved us" (Rom. 8:28, 37).

In my own life, the homosexual struggle was minimal. In late adolescence and young adulthood I was in an all-male seminary environment. It was during this time of my life that I experienced homosexual feelings and thoughts. It was less a sexual struggle than an emotional one. As I look back upon my own life, I realize that during this period of time I was attracted to other males who seemed more secure and confident of their masculinity. It was this which I was really attracted to and admired. This often made me feel a strong emotional (bordering on sexual) attraction to these males. In retrospect I realize that while I rejected such feelings in myself I went on to achieve the very self-acceptance and emotional integration which I admired in others. As a result, the "homosexual" struggle did not need to be enacted and it was soon put to rest as a life-dominating preoccupation.

SIX STAGES OF HOMOSEXUAL DEVELOPMENT
As I put together the thinking of many experts whom I have consulted in the area of homosexual development, and as I examine my own clinical experience with the many people I have personally counseled in Christian psychotherapy, worked with and consulted with through our group ministry, I have been able to identify six stages of homosexual development.

In counseling the overcomer it is important that you understand your overcomer in relation to these stages. It is going to help him come to an important awareness and insight about himself as a person as well as shed light about the family in which he grew up. I believe that it will bless him richly.

Low Self-Esteem (LSE) is the first stage. It arises from some form of dysfunctional family upbringing. It has to do with an inability to accept oneself (one's SELF) emotionally. Having one's emotions and feelings acknowledged, understood, accepted, and responded to gives the young child an adequate and acceptable SELF or Self-Esteem. It is a sense of how I feel about myself, my worth, my significance, my lovableness, adequacy, etc. This is for every child a major emotional integration or achievement in the life-cycle of the sense of SELF, self-love, self-worth, or self-esteem. When an adequate sense of SELF is not achieved, low self-esteem results. Renewing an intimacy with and acceptance of one's emotional life is a major step in the healing of homosexuality. Acceptance of one's inner self or feelings is fundamental to all emotional healing and growth for a person who has experienced a dysfunctional family background.

Gender Emptiness (GE) is the second stage. When there is a foundation of LSE, the child is emotionally vulnerable in many ways. If a father calls his son a sissy, rejects him, and refuses to associate with him; when male peers tease or make fun of the LSE boy, or he fails at male-related activities and develops a fear of male aggressiveness, GE results. GE is a gender identity insecurity.

The young child begins to develop an inner insecurity and uncertainty that he is male or masculine enough. Because he experienced humiliation, intimidation, fear, anxiety, embarrassment, shame, criticism, poor modeling or insufficient modeling, lack of opportunity to experience success, acceptance, belonging with his same gender parent and peers, gender identity security is arrested. All of these and other factors conspire to produce an inner complex of feelings which causes a self-rejection or lack of intimacy with oneself as a male person.

Gender self-acceptance as a unique male or female, with all his or her limitations and assets, is a major step in the healing of homosexuality.

Gender Attraction (GA) is the third stage in the development of homosexuality. Because the young preadolescent is GE or gender identity insecure, he experiences an emotional deprivation which makes him very needy or hungry for other males to accept, approve, and be close to him. While he may feel quite comfortable and even secure with the opposite sex in a social sense, he continues to feel somewhat hyper-interested in the same gender. The young male overcomer looks to other males for his identity since his own is insecure. He forms an attraction and an attachment to other same gender persons in an intense way.

What most boys take for granted and assimilate as a matter of ordinary development through affiliation and friendships with other peers, becomes a full-time preoccupation for the GE boy. Instead of companions, associations, and friendships with other boys, peers become objects of intense interest in terms of physical attraction (male features, build, aggressiveness, confidence, anatomy, etc.), and emotional attachment.

The GE boy has intense emotional feelings about other boys. He feels an emotional dependency characterized by jealousy, hurt, comparisons, intense closeness, falling in love, and emotional excitement. He wants another boy to love him, single him out, and make him the object of his exclusive attention and affection. This need for emotional intimacy and attachment becomes a major underlying dynamic of the homosexual preoccupation.

Sexual Attraction (SA) is the fourth stage. LSE led to GE and GE led to GA. Now in adolescence GA easily becomes SA.

All those attractive features with which the GE-GA boy identifies and seeks for himself now become sexualized and eroticized.

Sexual attraction involves the arousal of sexual feelings concerning what is highly desirable and with which he wants intimacy and contact. Because same gender emotional intimacy and identification were arrested, deprived, denied, unachieved with the same gender parent and peer, the GE-GA boy finds himself sexually attracted to the same gender.

Homosexual Reinforcement (HR) is the next stage. The LSE-GE-GA-SA young overcomer begins to engage in those sexual activities which reinforce and habituate his homosexual disorientation. He begins to masturbate with continuous homosexual or male fantasies; he buys pornography, goes to erotic bookstores, watches erotic videos, and reads erotic literature. He begins seeking other same gender people with whom he forms emotional attachments and becomes sexually involved; he begins to become a compulsive visual addict, looking for handsome and attractive males wherever he goes.

Homosexual Identity (HI) is the final stage in the development of the homosexual disorientation. Because he must come to some peace about his sexual identity and orientation, he begins to justify his lifestyle of homosexual behavior and forms an identity as a homosexual or "gay" person. Once this identity is consolidated and he begins to associate with a gay community and companions, he becomes very defensive about his choice and will not allow anyone (family, pastors, friends) to convince him of a change in his identity. That change will only come about for compelling personal reasons and the work of the Holy Spirit in his life.

Helping your overcomer understand himself in terms of this six-stage development produces an important awareness and insight about the causes of his homosexual disorientation. It helps him come to grips with the reality that homosexuality is a disorientation (as unpleasant as that may be) and that the gay world is a delusion of self-deception and lies, fabricated and supported by society in order to support a carnal and sinful lifestyle.

NOTE: Most of this chapter is written in the second person singular to illustrate how to share these stages as a personal teaching to your overcomer. After each stage there are exercises to personalize your overcomer's experience.

Stage One: Low Self-Esteem

The first stage is the foundation stage that is found in most, if not all psychological, emotional problems in personality in adult life. This is the stage in which the overcomer's self-esteem was threatened, weakened, and poorly established. It arises in the context of a dysfunctional family; a family where feelings are often ignored, unspoken, unexpressed and/or confused. It has been said that the three rules of a dysfunctional family are, "Don't feel, don't talk about your feelings, don't trust others or your feelings." In such a family low self-esteem is formed; a root condition I find in all Christians struggling to overcome homosexuality.

The roots of LSE begin to form right from birth. This is why overcomers sometimes feel that they have felt homosexual from the start. Some overcomers may have experienced primitive biological traumas to their self-esteem, as, for instance, when a parent desires a child of the opposite sex or when the child is not wanted at all.

In the mysterious linkage between the emotional-mental condition of the pregnant mother and her in utero biological environment, such feelings and desires are transmitted to the growing fetus. In another situation, one overcomer's mother died at childbirth, leaving him with a grief-stricken and guilt-producing father and a complete lack of mothering in the early stages of life.

But aside from these in utero and traumatic beginnings, LSE usually results from the dysfunctional, unstable family and parental environment in this early period of life. In one way or another, the family or marriage is dysfunctional and LSE begins to develop.

What is self-esteem and low self-esteem? How does self-esteem normally develop? How does it become threatened and weakened? How does LSE relate to the development of homosexuality? These are the first issues that you should help your overcomer understand from his or her early childhood. At that stage of life, he may not recall specific events but rather he may come to understand an "atmosphere" or "climate" that pervaded his home. He can find this out by talking to his parents, his brothers and sisters or relatives, by examining photos from childhood, by visiting his old home neighborhood, by helping him to picture himself in childhood and capture his old feelings and impressions. Have him begin to record his impressions in a journal or diary. Sit with him as you both discuss photos from his past, asking him questions and giving him your impressions.

> What have you heard about the time before you were born? What was happening in your family, in the neighborhood, the world? What was the community and house like that you lived in? Describe these as ways of jogging your memory.
>
> What is your earliest memory? Tell some stories about events you can remember from the period when you were under five.

What were your parents like? What are some dominant impressions about them? Any quick impressions of your mother or father?

What were they going through financially?

What feelings arise as you think and recall this time of life?

Bob's Journal

The only thing I personally remember is from a photo of my family. We were in front of our house in Brooklyn. I was on my mother's lap with my two older sisters kneeling in front. My father stood behind my mother. That might be significant in itself. He was very handsome; like someone who I (now that I am an adult) might be attracted to. He had curly black hair and a nicely trimmed mustache. He had a nice build, even white teeth, and was very masculine looking. All things that attract me now.

I must have been about three or four years old. My sisters are about six and eight. My parents are in their mid-to-late thirties. I am the youngest. What does that mean in terms of the birth order? What is different or special about the youngest child; the youngest male child with two older sisters? Later I found out that my mother lost a stillborn child just before me. He was a boy. I wondered about that. How did that affect my mother and father? What kinds of feelings were they having when my mother became pregnant with me after losing that child? Did they really want another child? What about a boy child? How did my father feel?

We lived in Brooklyn, New York at this time. I don't remember too much about the place where we lived except that it was an apartment house with lots of neighbors and noise. I get the feeling that I was protected from this "rough" environment by my mother. I apparently spent a lot of time in the apartment with her. My sisters and father were away a lot it seemed. My mom and I did a lot together, so I'm told. I slept in the same room as my parents because it was a two-bedroom apartment and my sisters had their own room.

My mom was excitable and loud; my dad quiet and complaining. These were some early impressions of them that still seem true today. They both complained about not having enough money and my mother "demeaned" my father about this as the man who was supposed to be a good provider. My oldest sister said that we were poor. I guess I had just entered kindergarten when we moved to Connecticut.

My mother and sisters said that I was a good baby. I guess I sort of had three mothers since they all took care of me and somewhat still have that attitude toward me today. From the photo and from later events I got the impression that my father was both sort of special (the only adult male with three "conspiring" women) and also the object of some hidden derision and criticism behind his back, mostly from my mother. Even from this stage I feel like my mother was not satisfied with my father.

What about Your Self-Esteem?

Self-esteem is the way you feel about yourself. Self-Image is the way you think about yourself. In reality, how you feel about yourself (Self-Esteem) is that deep, underlying sense of how significant, confident, and worthwhile you feel about yourself and is more important to your emotional well-being than your self-image (how others see you and you think of yourself). Self-esteem is the basis of your faith in yourself, hope in yourself, and love of yourself. When your self-faith, self-hope, and self-love are threatened or inadequate, you begin to relate to all of life with insecurity.

Nathaniel Branden says that self-esteem is "our experience of being competent to deal with the challenges of life and of being deserving of happiness. [It] is a function of our deepest feelings about ourselves; it is not a matter of particular skills or particular knowledge. It is certainly not a matter of how well liked we are. It is a matter of the extent to which we experience ourselves as appropriate to life and the requirements of life. [It is an] experience that we are competent to live and worthy of happiness."[2]

When you let yourself feel (not think) how you feel about yourself, what "bounces" back at you? Filling in the following sentence can help you get in touch with how you feel about yourself: "I feel ____ about myself." Say it to yourself four more times slowly and see what word or words comes to mind. What do you get? What bounces back at you?

Self-esteem has to do with feelings about yourself; about your SELF. A person with good self-esteem gets a "bounce back" of feelings of being valued, worthwhile, loved, cherished, trusted, important to HIMSELF, from HIMSELF.

Close your eyes and say each of these:

I am meaningful! (feel what happens)

I am worthwhile.

I like myself.

I am valuable.

I am important.

What bounces back at you? Do you really believe and feel these things about yourself?

When Bob did these exercises he experienced uncertainty, confusion, and a strange emptiness. He found it difficult to really feel himself at all. He felt something was missing. He can connect these feelings with this early stage of life and in his family generally. Many times he felt this way in his family.

At this early stage of life when self-esteem is developing, parents are the mirrors in which Bob looked to see what he first felt about himself. And what did he see and feel when he looked into his parental mirrors? Bob saw a disinterest, a disregard, a lack of connectedness, and a distant feeling of uncaring from his father. He saw a mechanical caregiving from his mother. Even in the photo Bob has the impression that his mother is fretting and that he is far away from his father.

What do you see when you look into your parental mirrors? What did you see then? What do you still see now? Take a few moments and reflect on this early stage. Let the Holy Spirit lead you into deep understanding of your emotional life at this stage of self-esteem development. Do you feel inadequate, unimportant, victimized, defeated, or afraid?

Stage Two: Gender Emptiness

Low self-esteem (LSE) is the foundation of the homosexual disorientation. LSE is the general condition and vulnerability which sets up the child to receive the special vulnerability called Gender Emptiness (GE).

When a child experiences an inadequacy of family love

which the Bible calls *storgē* (stor-gay) love, in those early, emotionally vulnerable years of life, he becomes vulnerable to being emotionally wounded in his gender security and identity. For overcomers, this special emotional wounding becomes focused on the area of his male identity and security. I call this Gender Emptiness. LSE (Low Self-esteem) is the foundation of GE (Gender Emptiness).

Somewhere between the ages of four and seven or eight, you experienced a number of negative events and feelings, especially gender-related feelings, which began to develop a gender insecurity and woundedness. These events and feelings were primarily experienced in the presence of your father (or the lack of a father) at this early stage.

Some things happened at this early age which left you with the beginning of gender uncertainty and insecurity. Some strong emotionally charged events took place which impacted you in very significant ways. These events-into-feeling experiences were charged with self-feelings of anger, guilt, self-pity, remorse, sadness, loss, hurt, rejection, and many others. This accumulation of feelings formed a complex or nest of wounded emotions which I have come to call the Deprivation Complex. Later I will identify fifteen wounded emotions or "needles" and several defenses or "guards" which make up this deprivation complex or wounded area. This wounded emotional area, buried in the unconscious, sets you up to be obsessed with same-sex needs and interests; with unfulfilled "homo-emotional" longings and hunger which I call Gender Emptiness.

Do you feel that you are obsessed with other males? You can't stop noticing them. You find yourself watching males incessantly. Attractive males seem to be everywhere. Images of them float through your mind continuously. They are in your dreams and fantasies. They accompany your masturbation. You look at them on videos, on television, and in the movies. They always seem to draw your attention. It is an obsession!

What is it that forms this obsession with the same sex? It is that unformed love-bond with your father (that first mysterious, emotionally charged male) which works itself into an inner "homo-emotional" hunger and emptiness. It becomes an inner, obsessive, emotional message which says over-and-over again:

I must be accepted by a man.

I must be loved by a man.

I must be noticed by a man.

I have to be close and intimate with a man.

I must fill this hunger to be emotionally connected to a man.

I must find a man who will love me.

I must prove that I am worthy of a man's love.

I must prove that I am acceptable to a man.

I must be possessed by a man.

I must fill this emptiness with a man.

I must redo and reexperience anew these feelings of anger, sadness, fear, loss, pain, hurt, acceptance, rejection, guilt, and grief with a man.

I must be held by a man.

I must be emotionally and physically close and embraced by a man.

Because of your father's absence, harshness, disinterest, perceived rejection, or distance from you as a child, you were unable to bond with him in a way which settled your "homo-emotional" needs. As a result, you were unable to take from him an adequate male self-image because you were unable or unwilling to identify with this first important male in your life.

Why is it that other men who have had harsh or remote fathers do not develop this Gender Emptiness; this Deprivation Complex, this homosexual obsession? Because the other factors did not accumulate and conspire to rob them of their sense of masculine identity. They were probably accepted by their peers, involved with competitive sports, and had a more aggressive temperament. Perhaps they did not have an early sexual exploitative experience; they didn't become overly attached to their mothers; they did not have medical or physical problems, etc.

But for you, these other factors conspired to reinforce the Gender Emptiness. For instance, your mother may have been overprotective, overdominating, seductive, immature, devouring, or tyrannical. You may have found yourself overly enmeshed with your mom in dependency. At the same time you were also overly enmeshed with your dad in defiance, fear, and hatred. Both entanglements prevented you from developing suitable male security for which Gender Empty people hunger. An internal emotional wall went up between your INNER CHILD and your INNER PARENT, causing a gender hunger; a Gender Emptiness.

Bob's Journal

My father worked a lot and came home very late in the evening when I was this age. I didn't even know what kind of work he did for quite some time. I didn't see him very much. He was there but he wasn't there at the same time. I knew he was a presence in the house, but I never connected with him personally or emotionally. It was strange. There he was, the man called "father," but I never experienced what was supposed to happen between a father and a son, whatever that is.

On weekends he was off by himself. He did very little with the family. My mother complained about this a lot. When he came home in the evening from work, I guess I was asleep most of the time, only to find him absent the next morning.

My God, what a distant figure he was. I never realized how remote he was for a lot of my life. I took it for granted that he was a nonperson; that we had no relationship. This made him so mysterious and interesting. I felt very emotionally interested in him in almost a nostalgic, sad sort of way, but emotionally distant from him all at the same time. It makes me realize that I have such deep, conflicting feelings about my father. Both love and hate; both interest and disregard; both longing to know him and not wanting to know him for some reason. It hurts inside to think that I never really knew who my father was; I never got to know the man. How could I become a man if I couldn't know this man, my father? Dad, I wish I knew you! I wish I could get to know you all over again! I wish we could start a new relationship! Dad, I miss not knowing you; I miss you! Dad, who are you?

I can see how this same nostalgic, sad, deeply felt conflicting set of feelings is always going on within me when I get emotionally interested and involved with a man. It's as if I am "doomed" to have to reexperience this over and over again until I get it settled and fulfilled and resolved. Every time I get this "empty" feeling I feel drawn to find a man who will love me. It's like a "possession" that comes over me. I must find a man to want me!

Excuse the emotion! As I thought about my father, it really got to me for a while.

Well, anyway, now I have to admit something that is embarrassing to me. When my father would come home at night (remember, I slept in the same room as my parents), I used to watch him undress while I pretended I was asleep.

I don't know why this fascinated me so much, but it did. Seeing him naked was exciting. You know, come to think of it, I now realize why it excited me. Seeing him naked was like getting to know the real person; a person who I didn't know at all; a person who wouldn't let me know him at all. Seeing him naked was seeing him vulnerable and real. This was emotionally charged for me.

I guess it was a sexual excitement I was feeling though I hardly realized it at the time. I know it really became sexual when I would watch my parents engaging in sexual intercourse.

Now I realize this wasn't so good for me to witness. This exposed me to more than a seven- or eight-year-old should be seeing. In reality, I guess you could call it a form of sexual abuse.

I was also fascinated by my father's masculine build. His body hair and manly appearance were a curiosity to me. I can remember this being so from when I was very young. Maybe this strong interest in his male characteristics was due to the fact that I felt so unlike him. I was more often associated with and in the company of my mother and sisters. I guess I really longed to be like him, if he had only given me a chance to ease up to him a little and identify with him. Instead, I was always around my mother and sisters and he remained so remote from me.

Once, I guess it was when I was around eight years old, he took me to a carnival. I wonder how my mother got him to do that? I remember how uncomfortable I felt with him. It was like being with a stranger because that's what he was to me. I think I was afraid to be with him because he didn't seem sensitive to my needs like my mother and sisters were. They were always looking out for me and serving me.

I always felt like I was a nuisance to him. He treated me as if I were an unavoidable obligation. Well, anyway, while we were at the carnival, I had to go to the bathroom. Maybe just being with him made me want to urinate out of fear. In any case, I told him this several times. In his usual way, he ignored me. Finally, I couldn't hold it in any longer and I wet my pants. When he discovered it he got angry at me and began insulting me.

This incident stands out so clearly that I am sure that it must be the most significant event or symbolic type of event that affected my gender emptiness feeling. It made me hate him and feel very afraid of him. After that, I refused to go with him or do anything with him again. I really can feel the hate and disappointment I felt with him. I think I said inside myself that I would never like him again. I think I can almost literally feel that wall go up between us from that time on. This one very powerful incident made me feel that my father (all men) was to be feared; that he (all men) was cruel, insensitive, hurtful, and bad. I didn't trust him (all men) from that time on. I'm sure about it.

What about Your Gender Emptiness?

How did your father treat you?

Can you recall times spent with him at this stage?

What kind of a man was he?

Can you remember incidents when you felt hurt, rejected, unaccepted, or mistreated by him?

Was fear, anger, and hurt part of your fear of him?

Did he show you affection?

Did you feel affection toward him?

What did he criticize you about?

What role did your mother and siblings play in relation to the way your father treated you?

What were some early feelings of GE or insecurity in your identity as a male?

Take a few moments and compare your answers to the above questions with the thirteen "I must" statements which make up the homosexual obsession we spoke of earlier. How do you see what happened with your father compared to your obsessive need to be accepted by and loved by a man today?

It would be most worthwhile if you would take the time to write out some of the events of this stage. Often, my clients in therapy find that the Holy Spirit will be present in the writing of their life story and use it as a time of deep feeling, insight, and healing.

Stage Three: Gender Attraction

During the preadolescent years of nine through twelve, you should have experienced friendship love (the Bible calls it *phileo*) with siblings and especially peers of the same sex (grades three through eight). Since you experienced GE though, it is likely that you were uncomfortable with same-sex peers because you did not feel adequate around them or equal to them or their activities and attitudes.

Athletics, in which you had to be a competing male among males, was probably frightening to you and something you may have avoided. When you had to participate with your peers you very likely received further rejection and unacceptance. This undoubtedly reinforced your GE feelings and exaggerated the deprivation complex.

At the same time, the child with LSE and GE finds himself very interested in males because there is a hunger, a deprivation in him to fill the male emptiness he has experienced. He desperately needs their acceptance and approval. So, there you were, both fearing and attracted to males at the same time. You were in an approach/avoidance dilemma. On the one hand, you felt the need to avoid males because you feared being exposed as less adequate. On the other, you felt an obsessive drawing to them in order to win their approval and acceptance. It was as if you could not overcome the fear until you made contact with the feared object.

Certain fixed ideas about masculinity began to develop. You found yourself looking at certain male characteristics as symbols of what it means to be a man. You found yourself attracted to males who had these characteristics, such as broad shoulders, dark hair, hairiness, athletic ability, toughness, unemotional, and coarse. These things are found to be interesting, even exciting. You became attracted to them and fascinated with them. You have gone from fear and anxiety to fascination and attraction. GE has become GA (Gender Attraction).

Bob's Journal

Since I didn't have brothers and was used to being around women, I tended to feel safer and more comfortable around girls. Girls were not sexually attractive to me. Somehow I just couldn't think of girls that way even though boys made sexual comments about them. To be sexually interesting, girls had to be mysterious and unknown, but for me, that was not the case. I had spent a lot of time with my mother and sisters and therefore they were familiar to me. I felt like I identified with them and was one of them even though I clearly knew that I was a boy.

On the other hand, boys were a mystery to me. Boys were unknown to me. I was not at home with them and therefore they became objects of intense interest. At this point boys were not sexually interesting to me. Rather, I just felt distant from them and wanted so much to be one of them. They interested me so much.

Of course, if I were to see a boy naked in a locker room, I would have a strange and curious interest in him sexually. I didn't want to feel that way but I recognized that it was happening and I didn't feel like I could do much about it. I would have a hard time taking my eyes off of a naked boy and later found myself thinking about what I had seen over and over again. It really embarrassed me whenever I realized that I was developing an erection in these situations and so I quickly learned to avoid locker room situations.

Other boys also treated me as different, I guess. I wasn't very good at sports; I had the ability but not the confidence. Where other boys would aggressively swear off their errors, I would become very upset with myself and feel defeated emotionally. Instead I excelled at academics. My teachers all liked me. The admiration of teachers did not make me popular with my male peer group and forced me to be further identified with the girls in class who also excelled academically.

I had one male friend who was particularly close to me. I

remember how good it felt to have someone who really wanted to be with me. It felt great when he called me up and asked me to go somewhere with him or visit with him. He showed me his father's pornography collection; an assortment of cartoon books, playing cards, and magazines. This was our secret. Then he told me about masturbation. We compared penises once. He was ashamed of his small size. Once while we were wrestling I got an erection and he knew it. I think he was a little afraid of me and his own reaction from then on. These were some of the first homosexual stirrings in me.

Since I wasn't so bad looking, I was popular with girls. My sisters thought I was really cute and made a big deal over me. I went to some parties where we kissed and necked and it felt terrific. For a while it put to rest my inadequate feelings about masculinity. In fact, I became so comfortable with the good feelings I had from these early heterosocial experiences that I became emotionally dependent on one girl. Her parents thought it too much for kids our age and made us break it off.

What about Your Gender Attraction?

Do you remember comparing yourself with other boys?

Do you remember specific boys that you looked up to? Why?

What about your early relationship with your brother(s)?

What was your attitude toward and ability in athletics?

What did you feel about getting hurt or getting into fights?

When you were with boys or friends, what role did you play?

Did you have girlfriends?

Did you have crushes on other boys?

What characteristics in boys did you associate with maleness?

Reflect on and write about the answers to these questions. Can you see some of the same themes from the GE stage operating in this stage of the homosexual development?

Stage Four: Sexual Attraction

During this stage (ages twelve–seventeen, junior high–high school) it is likely that you began to get romantic crushes on males and experienced feelings of "falling in love." These are the signs that GA (Gender Attraction) is becoming SA (Sexual Attraction). Since you are now an adolescent, you have become a sexual person. You experience the normal feelings of sexual and erotic stirrings.

As you began to become biologically and hormonally a sexual person, the LSE, GE, GA develops into SA or Sexual Attraction. Emotionally, you are still feeling undeveloped in your identity as a male. That GE has now been reinforced through GA toward the same sex. It is therefore only "natural" that the same sex will become the object of your sexual interest and attraction. Those gender attractive characteristics which were objects of interest and admiration in GA, now become fixed as sexualized characteristics (broad shoulders, hairiness, dark hair, etc.). What was fear and excitement in the LSE, GE stages; fascination and interest in the GA stage, becomes sexualized and erotic in the SA stage. You become hooked on males as sexualized objects of attraction.

Bob's Journal

I worked hard at hiding the homosexual feelings I was recognizing in myself. I became more withdrawn and distant. I hardly ever had moments of real laughter and spontaneity anymore because I saw myself so preoccupied with this unacceptable orientation. I started to masturbate with homosexual fantasies and images. I collected some heterosexual pornography, though it was really the males I was interested in seeing in these pictures. Collecting gay pornography would have forced me to admit to myself that I was gay.

Once, my high school French club took a trip to Canada to be in a French-speaking environment and to practice using our French. It was one of the first times I shared close quarters with another male. The guy I roomed with was someone who had told me that he thought he was gay some months before. I guess both of us felt somewhat attracted to each other since we were able to build a bond over the fact that we had mutually shared having homosexual feelings. We probably both entertained fantasies about sharing a room on this trip, and when we were given the choice to choose our roommate, we chose each other.

The nights we were in Canada we "experimented" sexually. We got in bed, held each other, kissed a little and engaged in mutual masturbation. That was all, but it was the first homosexual experience for each of us and it felt exciting, relieving, and frightening all at the same time. It was frightening for me because, as I said before, I really didn't want to see myself as someone gay. For the next two years this guy and I got together sexually about eight or ten other times.

My family had become active in a good biblical church around this time and we went to church regularly. My dad was changing in some nice ways toward my mom and me as a result of his born-again experience. He was more kind, open, and talkative. He spent more time with the family. My sisters were both out of the house by now. In church I heard a few references to homosexual sin, but no one ever suggested that you could do anything about it. It was mostly a message of condemnation.

Toward the end of my senior year in high school, our church youth group went to a regional youth rally in another city. There was a conference speaker there who gave a very stirring testimony about having been a former homosexual. He really captured my attention though I didn't let anyone know that I had a special reason for being interested. He planted the thought and the desire, by the Holy Spirit, that I should and could do something to change my homosexuality.

He invited people to come and speak with him privately and in an inconspicuous way. Though I was very nervous about talking with him, I felt led by the Holy Spirit to do so. I talked, or should I say mostly cried, for almost two hours. At the end of our conversation he led me in the sinner's prayer and I turned my life and my problem with homosexuality over to God. He also said that he would send me information about a local ministry which would support me in overcoming homosexuality.

When I went home after the conference I felt as if a tremendous weight had been lifted from me. For seven or eight months after that, right up until the end of my first semester at college, I can honestly say that I felt completely delivered of homosexual desires and attractions. Then it began all over again!

Stage Five: Homosexual Reinforcement

During the ages of approximately eighteen to twenty-four, or young adulthood, the struggle with sexual desires and feelings intensifies. Some people who have experienced the LSE, GE, GA, SA development may continue to feel sexual desires in a private preoccupation with fantasies, pornography, and visual indulgences. Others may become more public and promiscuous, frequenting bars, cruising areas, bath houses, restrooms, or even committing to a one-on-one relationship with another gay person. This is a time when your sexual identity and orientation is reinforced by homosexual behavior of one kind or another in the usual course of things.

Bob's Journal

After my conversion experience at the conference I became active in church and in the Christian fellowship at college. It was in that fellowship that I met Carl. He was about my age and very good looking though somewhat effeminate. It wasn't long before we became acquainted and admitted to each other that we were struggling with the big "H," as we heard it referred to.

At first it was good to share our mutual problem. We were both feeling strong about overcoming it since we were both committed Christians. Gradually our walk with the Lord started to take a backseat to our emotional dependency on each other. We spent a lot of time together in what felt like a very special, caring relationship. There was no sexual activity between us and we even talked about setting up a college-based ministry for other Christian overcomers. We spoke with the college chaplain and we had his support.

I guess we both started to get a little careless and reckless. We started to have very sensitive and emotional talks, always ending with a "friendly" embrace. One night we added drinking to our talking and ended up sexually involved with one another. At first we dismissed it as an accident that would never happen again. But it did. We both knew we were sinning, but we seemed addicted to each other. That went on for a whole semester and the idea of a ministry got completely lost in the process.

By our sophomore year Carl decided to end the relationship because he had gotten really serious with the Lord and wanted to go to Bible school. I had such a strong emotional attachment to Carl by now that when he told me he wanted an end to our relationship I was depressed for weeks. I almost flunked out of school.

I also began to dislike myself intensely and was very angry at God for preferring Carl over me and for letting me down. I started cruising bars in defiance and anger; something that was really out of character for me. This only made me hate myself even more and deepened my depression. I ended up making two suicide attempts that year, one more serious than the other.

Because of the suicide attempts, the college chaplain referred me to a Christian counselor. Praise God! This was the beginning of some very important help that I needed. Someone has said, "God will not let you off, God will not let you go, God will not let you down." I was starting to feel His strong presence in my life once again.

What about Your Homosexual Reinforcement?

You can see the emotional links that have been made in the chain from LSE (Low Self-Esteem), GE (Gender Emptiness), GA (Gender Attraction), SA (Sexual Attraction), to HR, Homosexual Reinforcement. Link by link, you have attempted to meet your earliest needs for affection, appreciation, self-worth, self-significance, confidence, and masculine security (LSE-GE) through your closeness, attraction, and sexualized association with other males (GA-SA). As these needs are eroticized in fantasy or fact, a pattern of homosexual thinking, attraction, and behavior is established.

Michael Saia says,

> Most homosexually oriented men do not enter relationships with other men just to have sex. Rather, they are trying to fulfill their needs for unconditional love and a sense of identity. But sex often plays a part in these relationships, and after awhile confusion may occur. The man will begin to think sex will meet his basic needs, so he attempts to satisfy his needs in that way. Since sex is such a

powerful, pleasurable experience, it can quickly reinforce any behavior associated with it. This is how habit patterns of thinking (sexualization) and behavior (promiscuity) can so quickly become entrenched in the homosexual's life.[3]

Reflect on these questions:
Have you ended all former homosexual relationships?
Are you still associating with gays, going to bars, or cruising?
Have you held onto things which remind you of the past, such as photos, letters, music, clothes?
Are you still living with a former gay friend?
In what other ways are you reinforcing homosexuality?
How has God spoken to you about putting an end to this lifestyle?

Stage Six: Homosexual Identity

By the time a person is age twenty-five through thirty-five, he senses a strong internal desire to settle and consolidate his identity in all areas of life. He wants to be done with asking "Who am I?" which is really a developmental task that should be completed around late adolescence. He wants to get on with living. He desires to settle his career and his unfinished family business with his parents and siblings. He wants to establish meaningful social relationships. He seeks to have a meaningful relationship with God. He especially desires to consolidate and integrate his gender identity. In fact, he is reaching the outer limits of settling his gender and sexual identity.

Bob's Journal

After my suicide attempts I started counseling with a Christian counselor. I met with him regularly right through to the end of my college career. Counseling really helped me to pull myself together emotionally, psychologically, and spiritually.

I graduated as a language education teacher and now teach high school. I find my work mostly rewarding. Counseling helped me to see that overcoming homosexuality has a lot to do with such things as establishing a rewarding career, improving my relationship with my parents, getting involved in my church, and developing a network of good, supportive, Christian friends of both sexes. I also got active in a support ministry for overcomers. All these things together have helped me to do that internal and external work which is needed to overcome homosexuality. I have seen tremendous changes in myself as a result of the way the Holy Spirit has been active through my counselor, my church fellowship, and the support ministry. I feel more healed now than ever in my life. I know that there is more to be done but I thank God for what He has already accomplished.

While I have not been involved sexually with anyone for over three years, I still have temptations and attractions. I really feel that I have gained control over them though, and by and large they are not a big hassle anymore. I feel so much more together emotionally.

Recently, I told my oldest sister all about my struggle. We had a couple of wonderful talks together. I'm also spending some real quality time with my father and have come to really understand what happened in his life. I haven't said a word about my homosexuality to either of my parents yet. I guess I'm still not ready for that.

I began to date a nice Christian woman and recently told her about my past. She was very understanding and accepting of me and wanted to learn more about it. I realize that I'm just feeling my way in this relationship and have to work on learning all over again what it is to be in a heterosocial relationship. I have trouble with closeness and emotional intimacy with her but we are working on it.

I have come closer to the Lord and I can't go one day without talking to Him and sharing myself with Him in a real and personal way. If I fail to spend time with Him for even a few days, I feel like I'm missing one of my very best friends. I praise Him for the way He continues to heal me and make me "confident of this, that He who has begun a good work in you will carry it on until the day of Jesus Christ" (Phil. 1:6).

What about Your Sexual Identity?

Write out the answers to these questions and discuss them with your counselor or special friend.

What sex do you most identify with now and in the past?

What would make you feel more secure in your anatomical sex, both feelings and physical?

How do you think most people perceive you sexually? What appears effeminate in your estimate?

Did you ever feel like you wanted to be the opposite sex? Did you ever act that way?

In your fantasies and past sexual behavior did you see yourself as the dominant or passive partner?

If your sexuality total is 100 percent, what percentage of your sexuality is homosexual? How much is heterosexual?

On a scale of 1 to 5 (5 = very strongly) how strongly do you want to change your homosexual disorientation?

FOR THE COUNSELOR

Bob never chose to be homosexual initially. Neither did your overcomer! It began in the early triangle of relationships which he had with his parents and especially with the first significant same-gender parent in his life. It was reinforced by peers and his environment. It may have been aggravated by pre-birth factors. Together, these coalesced into a conspiracy of elements which form the roots of LSE and GE. The emotional vulnerability of LSE became focused on his gender identity and security because of the poor love bond between him or her and the parent of the same gender. This formed the beginnings of GE. Feeling LSE and GE, the overcomer then attempted to fill that emptiness by a continuous gender attraction (GA) to other same gender people, which in adolescence became eroticized SA (Sexual Attraction). Later, that SA is reinforced through homosexual behavior of one kind or another and through emotional attachments. This HR is consolidated into an identity (HI) which could develop into a whole, justified, sinful lifestyle in the late twenties and thirties unless there is the conviction and desire to change.

When the overcomer is born again, the Holy Spirit convicts his heart and leads him to seek out the help to become an overcomer. Praise God!

You have prepared your overcomer with the four basic questions and the ten basic facts about homosexuality. You have prepared him spiritually. You have helped him to gain the understanding and insight into the causes and development of homosexuality.

I would suggest that you carefully use the material in this chapter to understand the emotional and psychological roots of homosexuality. Visualize yourself as unwrapping the six layers of homosexuality starting with stage six.

First, your overcomer must begin to disassociate with "gay" or "homosexual." He must not only do this behaviorally (e.g., no more gay bars, etc.), but emotionally. He must begin to see himself as heterosexual. He might do this by beginning to associate with more heterosexual men and their activities more frequently.

Second, he must make significant efforts to discontinue all homosexual reinforcements. Masturbation with homosexual imagery, gay friendships, emotional attachments, and pornography are important reinforcers that he must discontinue (see next chapter).

Third, he must work at reducing and eliminating sexual attraction. Several techniques will be suggested for dealing with temptation.

Fourth, gender attraction and fifth, gender emptiness will begin to change as he begins to experience himself as a man with self-confidence, security, and self-worth. His work on reducing intimacy anxiety with the opposite sex will also aid these changes.

Last, guide him in those efforts which contribute to his growth in self-esteem (emotionally, relationally, vocationally, educationally, spiritually).

Is your overcomer ready to take the first active steps? Here is what he must do to begin to change.

---

1. Ed Hurst, *Development and Treatment of Homosexuality* (Minneapolis: Outpost, n.d.), 1.

2. Nathaniel Brandon, *To See What I See and Know What I Know: A Guide to Self-Discovery.* (New York: Bantam, 1985), 10.

3. Michael Saia, *Counseling the Homosexual* (Minneapolis: Bethany, 1988), 56.

CHAPTER FIVE

WHAT DO I HAVE TO DO TO CHANGE?

"What do I have to do to change?" every overcomer asks. Changing homosexuality can be viewed as having to do with two general areas of change.

First, it has to do with making constructive, positive changes in his habitual ways of behaving and relating to his environment and especially the reduction of his homosexual outlets. These are the outer, external changes. Secondly, it has to do with experiencing healing in the way he perceives, thinks about, feels, and processes his inner life.

This internal change especially means rebuilding his self-esteem and self-image and changing the deprivation complex and defenses which I spoke of earlier. It also refers to removing or at least diminishing those boulders, rocks, and pebbles which have gotten in the stream of the heterosexual developmental flow.

The external changes are more visible, tangible, and generally more easily accomplished in a shorter time. The internal personality changes are more imperceptible, more intangible, and usually take longer to heal through a process of gradual change. Both need the working of the Spirit of Christ in your overcomer to be effectively accomplished.

REALISTIC CHANGE: WHAT IS IT?

Is complete and total change possible? Can a person expect to arrive at a time when he will not even retain a memory of homosexual feelings or thinking? Are all things possible with God? Yes! Yes! God is certainly able to eliminate every trace of homosexual interest and desire in a person. What is impossible with man is possible with God.

But let me anchor these words about complete change in God's Word. The Bible teaches us that believers have two natures. One is the "old man" or carnal nature which we all inherit from Adam. The other is the "new man" or regenerated nature which is born in us when we are saved through faith in Christ Jesus the Lord. "If any man be in Christ, he is a new creature" (2 Cor. 5:17, KJV).

The old nature is never completely eradicated, even though the new nature gives us victory over this sin-prone old man. This victory comes as the overcomer yields to the Holy Spirit daily and moment by moment, even though the old nature continues to assert itself and is never completely overcome in this life.

What does this mean for the person who is overcoming homosexuality? My experience as a Christian therapist and ministry leader is that I have seen most overcomers experience a great degree of freedom from homosexuality. Over time they report an almost complete absence of homosexual thinking, feeling, and attraction. They are able to go on with their lives as "normal" in all respects with a very small "h" remaining. This means that they may still experience some homosexual feelings or interests from time to time; some temptations, but with a minimum of tension, conflict, or difficulty. As they yield these temptations to the Holy Spirit, they are easily dismissed and resisted. These temptations are there as "minimally bothersome" only.

Your goal for your overcomer is to trust God "who is able to do immeasurably more than all we ask or imagine according to His power that is at work within" (Eph. 3:20) your overcomer.

THE STRESS-RELIEF CYCLE
One of the most important experiences which the overcomer needs to recognize in himself is the way he manages and copes with emotional stress. The reason he continually finds himself slipping or falling into homosexual behavior of one

kind or another (aside from his fallen human nature) is related to his inability to effectively manage and cope with emotional stress, those things that stimulate and set him up for homosexual acting out. He needs to understand the operation of his stress-relief cycle (see diagram #1).

Diagram 1

The Stress-Relief Cycle

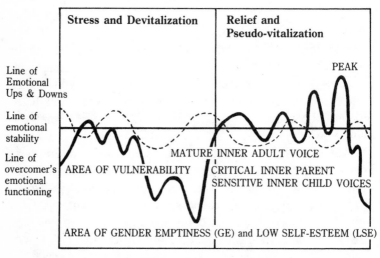

Think of the ideal way to manage one's emotional life as a lifeline of emotional stability. This is a steady, unwavering line of unchanging emotions. Of course, no one is like that in reality. We are all much more like the broken line of emotional ups and downs. Our emotional life goes up and down within a reasonably comfortable range day after day. It rarely goes very high or very low, or only for short periods of time. That's what most people are like who are not under a great deal of stress.

The overcomer is somewhat different. Because of his background in an emotionally dysfunctional family, he often experiences his emotional life as continuously operating below the line of "normal" emotional ups and downs. This is represented by the dark line. He finds himself in a chronic state of stress and devitalization. Devitalization means an emotional state of lifeless, depleted, unexcited, unhappy emptiness.

Sometimes he is near the "norm." Perhaps he is, at times, even at the norm of emotional stability. More often, however, he is functioning below it. The reason for this is because he has an underlying, undermining area of Gender Emptiness and Low Self-Esteem as well as an area of vulnerability because of his critical inner parent and sensitive inner child voices.

While he may keep himself functional most of the time because he can hear his rational mature adult voice, many times he is overwhelmed by the troubling and unhealed voices of his inner parent and child which set him up for homosexual acting out.

When he reaches, as he does periodically, a deep low of emotional pain, he escapes his emptiness by engaging in those homosexual outlets which bring relief and pseudo-vitalization. For a very short time, his indulgence in masturbation, pornography, exhibitionism, or sexual gratification relieves him of his emptiness and he experiences a peak of temporary and artificial aliveness or pseudovitalization.

This stress-relief cycle phenomenon is troublesome for overcomers and accounts for the most addictive aspects of homosexual behavior. When overcomers begin to effectively change their sensitive and critical inner voices, they will find themselves less addictive and will improve their self-esteem and gender identity security. This must take place with a simultaneous effort involving a number of external changes.

EXTERNAL CHANGES

What are the external changes? The external changes have to do with a number of practical things which begin to change homosexuality. Some of them will help your overcomer manage the most annoying and discouraging aspects of homosexuality. Some are personal; some are relational. Many of these can be enacted almost immediately. Instruct your overcomer in this way.

Seven Personal Changes

1. Adopt gender-appropriate clothes, appearance, talk, and behavior. If you are unable to determine this for yourself, let

someone whom you trust give you some honest feedback about these things. Perhaps your counselor can help. Some male overcomers have clothing, hairstyles, mannerisms, and behavior which are "gay" or even effeminate. Some women have masculine appearances and clothing. You can change much of this.

2. What about your physical health? Do you need to be tested for AIDS? Do you have other sexually related illnesses that need attention? What about your general health practices? Your dental, weight, exercise, and nutritional care all contribute to a good self-esteem and self-image.

3. Rid yourself of all pornographic materials! All erotic magazines, literature, videos, books, pictures, music, letters, or condoms should no longer be a part of your life. It may cost you something financially and emotionally to part with some of these items. The break with all of these things symbolizes a break with a former lifestyle and past and is an indication of a serious decision to change. Don't hold anything back! Get rid of it all; once and for all!

4. Begin to learn about homosexuality through reading. This is most important. Your mind has to understand many things so that you "do not conform any longer to the pattern of this world, but be transformed by the renewing of your mind" (Rom. 12:2).

There are many fine books and tapes available which will help you understand the dynamics of homosexuality. Remember, the truth can set you free! There is a list of resources at the end of this book.

5. Learn your triggers and setups! Overcomers are vulnerable to a number of people, events, and circumstances which act as "trigger mechanisms" and "setups" for homosexual feelings, thoughts, and desires. These are very important.

What do I mean by "triggers" and "setups"? Triggers are anything which directly stimulates sexual excitement or arousal. Erotic books, videos, music, TV programs, the use of alcohol or drugs, provocative clothing, cruising areas, gay bars, porno bookstores, malls, beaches, rest rooms and the like, are all triggers. They can trigger homosexuality because of their suggestiveness or provocativeness.

Setups are the people, events, or circumstances which provoke the deprivation complex, that wounded area of emotions and defenses which is at the root of homosexuality. Leisure time, vacations, changes in the seasons, holidays (especially Christmas and New Year's Eve), family gatherings, transitions (such as the end of a school year, the loss of a friend, the change of job or residence), are all potential setups. People who are rejecting, hard to get along with, emasculating, or demeaning are also setups.

Any of these events, people, or circumstances set you up to feel the same complex of deprived feelings; feelings of self-pity, self-rejection, anger, guilt, shame, sadness, inadequacy, self-condemnation, emptiness, bitterness, loneliness, fear, failure, weakness, ridicule, anxiety, lovelessness, helplessness, and victimization.

These were the very same feelings that initially formed your LSE and GE when you were a child. These are the same wounded feelings and defensive reactions which continue the homosexual compromise. It is probably evident to you that when setups and triggers occur together, it is almost inevitable that you will be severely tempted to seek out some homosexually related avenue of relief and release.

The setups and triggers are the external events, people, and circumstances which aggravate the internal deprivation complex of wounded emotions and defenses. Eliminating and avoiding the triggers; managing and coping with the setups more effectively; and learning how to tolerate and process your wounded emotions and defenses is at the very heart of healing homosexuality.

6. Temptations — whether of the imagination, visual, or relational — need to be managed and disciplined in positive, effective ways. Here are ten techniques for times of temptation.

Arm yourself with the Word of God. Begin to search the Scriptures for verses that you can memorize and use during times of temptation. Here are five powerful verses many overcomers use to break the devil's hold on their thoughts and feelings.

"I can do all things through Christ which strengtheneth me" (Phil. 4:13, KJV).

"Greater is He that is in you than he that is in the world" (1 John 4:4, KJV).

"Resist the devil, and he will flee from you" (James 4:7, KJV).

"If God is for us, who can be against us?" (Rom. 8:31)

"The Lord is near to all who call on Him, to all who call on Him in truth" (Ps. 145:18).

When these or similar verses are spoken silently or verbally, concentrating on the promises contained in them, and trusting that God stands behind His Word, temptations will weaken. Set yourself the goal of learning these five verses and their references this very week. Do it!

Walk through to the consequences. When you feel tempted to get involved with someone sexually (a fall), or engage in some homosexually related fantasy or material, you probably are caught up in the erotic feelings of the moment and are saturated in having and picturing the pleasure involved. You won't let yourself think about how you will feel after it's all over. You effectively block the guilt, the sense of shame, the sense of failure, discouragement, and sin of such an activity. To break the erotic "spell" you are under, walk your mind through to the consequences. Reflect on how you will feel later.

The rubber band technique. Place a rubber band on your wrist. Every time you catch yourself watching someone erotically or engaging in a fantasy, snap the band. This will cause a moderate stinging pain which serves as a shocking reminder of what you are doing. This should help you interrupt the "spell."

Paradoxical results is the use of humor, hyperbole, and exaggeration to produce paradoxical effects from those expected. Example: You notice a well-built, handsomely attractive man. You begin to idealize his features and take visual pleasure in him as you begin to watch him. Silently, though you can't actually hear it, you're saying, "What nice, muscular arms he has; what beautiful blue eyes and dark black hair he has; what gorgeous teeth and a strong masculine face he has." This secret thinking produces erotic feelings and reinforces homosexuality.

To counteract this, begin to exaggerate, amplify, ridicule, and overemphasize what you are saying to yourself. In the above example, you might say, "This man must be a Greek god. I've just got to go up and talk with him. I must get close to him or I'll absolutely die. If I can just get to know him, my whole life will be absolutely wonderful from now on. He is so perfect. If I could just touch him I know that I'll never be unhappy again. If I could just gaze into those liquid eyes of blue radiance, I will be in ecstasy forever."

Once you hear yourself objectively exaggerating your secret eroticized language, you should begin to see through the falseness of your thoughts and feelings and the temptation should diminish. The "spell" should break from realizing that you have been talking a foolishness to yourself. You will realize how you idolize and idealize men.

Turn away. When you notice an attractive person, your mind rapidly goes through several steps of self-seduction. Some of these steps are automatic; others are under your control and involve conscious choice. Learning about these steps and how to block them should help you break the visual attraction "spell." Here are the six steps:

a. *Visual Attraction.* This is automatic. You simply can't help but notice a man who is attractive to you. Certain features and body builds have become habitually attractive to you.

b. *Visual Attention.* This step is a choice step. You can decide to give this attractive person your attention or not. It is at this step that you must say turn away, and then, turn away quickly. Doing this quickly will begin to break your former habit of always giving an attractive person your visual attention.

c. *Visual Pleasure.* If you allow yourself to move into this third step, you will experience pleasure in looking at this attractive person. Remember, this step is also one where you can make a choice!

d. *Sexual Pleasure.* You will begin to experience some form of sexual arousal or excitement. This is almost always automatic, if you have allowed yourself to move through the first three steps.

e. *Desire for Encounter.* This is also mostly automatic. You will desire to either make actual contact with the person, or you will retain the eroticized memory of this person in your fantasy bank for later recall.

f. *Act to Encounter.* If the circumstances allow, you will act to encounter this person. This is also a choice.

You may be saying, "But this is an awful lot of self-control and work!" It may be, right now. The fact is, you are at a stage of having to break some well-established habits. There is no other way to do that than to do it! When done frequently and forcefully, you should find yourself—as you continue to do other things as well—experiencing freedom from the automatic visual attraction indulgence game.

Thought stopping-thought substitution. Two simple twin techniques to use (perhaps in combination with the rubber band) involve stopping a thought or fantasy by internally saying **STOP!** in a sharp and forceful manner. Then follow through by substituting an interesting thought which you know will engage your mind.

Listing the reasons against. When you are thinking about indulging a sexual pleasure, one of the most effective techniques for stopping the temptation is to list the reasons why doing so is to your disadvantage. Here is a sample list:
 — I will feel guilty afterward.
 — This will be a setback for me.
 — It won't really satisfy me anyway.
 — It is sinful.
 — It is destructive to my self-esteem and self-image.

Say these to yourself in order to weaken the power of temptation. This is one of the best temptation stoppers because it has to do with your self-esteem; something that is precious to you.

Symbolic questioning. When you are fantasizing or looking at an attractive person, realize that what you are thinking about or looking at are symbols of what you want for yourself. They are symbols of masculinity and maleness. Ask yourself, "What is it that I am attracted to? What does it symbolize? What does he have that I want? What is it that I feel I am missing? What do those dark eyes, good build, and nice teeth mean to me?"

Spoil or break the idol. Most of the excitement or erotic charge involved in your attraction to men is because you have idealized or idolized maleness. Consequently, certain images of masculinity have become idols of worship. Michelangelo

(reputed to be homosexual) actually constructed his male idol under the guise of religious art when he sculpted the famous statue of David standing in Florence, Italy. When you indulge a fantasy or your eyes on an attractive male, you are making maleness an idol. Learn to break this idol or spoil it by reminding yourself that this attractive person:
— looks sickly and pale when he is sick
— was a child once with parents who loved him
— can get greedy, selfish, miserable, angry, possessive
— is someone whom Christ died for
— will also be laid out in death someday
— is intended to go to heaven and be with God

Monitor your temptations. Keep a daily log for thirty or more days of five areas:
— Visual attractions and indulgences
— Erotic fantasies, daydreams, dreams
— Masturbation
— Sexual material which you use
— Sexual encounters (falls) or near encounters

See what effect this kind of saturation reporting has on your continuation of these things.

7. Manage your masturbation. Many Christian overcomers have a special problem with masturbation. They often find themselves in a compulsive habit of masturbation that continually makes them feel troubled, ashamed, out-of-control, and self-condemning.

Masturbation is the intentional stimulation of the genitals to arouse sexual excitement and pleasure for the purpose of reaching orgasm. For most adults, masturbation is an adolescent practice which should discontinue when the adult has married and replaces self-stimulation with heterosexual intercourse.

Masturbation is sinful because it often becomes the primary means of sexual gratification and because it is accompanied by erotic fantasies. Some overcomers are able to masturbate infrequently and without fantasies. However, most overcomers are unable to reduce its frequency and find it almost impossible to masturbate without some type of homosexual imagery. This results in a continuous cycle of sinful behavior.

Masturbation becomes an addictive habit because it combines physical pleasure with homosexual imagery. As a result, it becomes a substitute and symbolic sexual experience for many single men and women who struggle with homosexuality. For many, it is compulsively engaged in as frequently as several times daily as a means of releasing pressure and tension, during times of stress and depression, and to counteract loneliness, isolation, and emptiness. It is most compulsive in those who have learned to rely on themselves to provide sexual gratification and who are really fearful of and insecure in forming committed heterosexual, heterosocial relationships.

OVERCOMING THE HABIT OF MASTURBATION

A habit is something done repeatedly, without questioning it or challenging it. To overcome the habit of masturbation, a person must make a planned effort to challenge it or interfere with it as a compulsive, spontaneous habit.

First, you must want to change this habit. A sincere desire to change this sinful habit must be spoken to God in prayer. Tell God that you really want to end this habit, that you feel out of control with it, and that you are unable to do it without His help. Ask for this help, believing and trusting as you ask. Tell Him that you expect Him to give you the strength and self-discipline you need. You may need to pray in this way several times.

Second, begin to study and reflect on your habit of masturbation. Learn something about it. How frequently does it happen? Where and when does it happen? How are you feeling physically and emotionally at such times? For instance, one person discovered that he always masturbates late at night, in bed, when he is very tired. Another discovered that it always seems to occur when he is feeling empty and somewhat depressed.

Third, learn to use the following method to interfere with or break the habit of masturbation. It involves doing five things, which make up the acronym **HABIT**. These are five choices you must make.

1. **H** stands for hazardous situations. What are the hazardous circumstances and situations for you when masturbation usually takes place? For instance, does it occur whenever you

are in bed; or early in the morning when you shower; when you are bored and restless? These are your hazardous times. Being alert to these circumstances and changing those which you can should begin to interfere with the masturbation habit.

2. **A** stands for actions. What are you actually doing to stimulate yourself with your eyes, your hands, your body? You must make a decision to notice this and stop.

3. **B** stands for Bible verses. Use certain memorized Bible verses to strengthen your resolve and draw on God's help when you are tempted to masturbate. Look these verses up and consider memorizing them: Psalms 37:5; 46:1; Isaiah 26:3; Matthew 4:4, 7, 10; Romans 8:28; Philippians 4:13, 19.

4. **I** stands for intentions. Speak these words strongly within yourself: "I do not intend to masturbate because . . ."
- I don't want to sin.
- I don't like this image of myself.
- I am a new person in Christ.
- It is not good for my self-esteem.
- It makes me feel like a hypocrite and a phony.
- I have the self-control to overcome this habit.

5. **T** stands for thoughts. Consciously change your thoughts. The habit of masturbation is always stimulated by erotic, sexual thoughts. When such thoughts occur it is very important for you to bring "into captivity every thought to the obedience of Christ" (2 Cor. 10:5, KJV). An effective way to do this is to forcefully say stop! Then, begin to distract yourself with another activity or thought.

If you make the conscious attempt to use **HABIT,** you should be able to greatly diminish masturbation. God will surely strengthen and bless you for these efforts. Remember, "The Lord seeth not as man seeth; for man looketh on the outward appearance, but the Lord looketh on the heart" (1 Sam. 16:7, KJV).

The two-week challenge. Another very effective method for breaking the addictive masturbation cycle is to ask your overcomer to commit himself to the two-week challenge. That is, challenge him to not masturbate for two weeks. Tell him that he is forming a contract with you with these stipulations. Every time he wants to masturbate during this period of time, he should use HABIT. Each time he wants to masturbate he should take an attitude of "research" or study his need to maturbate. Ask him to really get to understand why he allows himself to masturbate.

During this two-week period, tell him that he must call you within twelve hours if he does break the challenge. Also, if at the end of two weeks he has not broken the challenge, you will take him to dinner or some such reward.

Tell him that if he makes the challenge, he will discover new strength and confidence in himself. This is the real importance of the challenge. He will realize that he does have the self-discipline and that he is not as weak as he may have thought.

Lastly, if he finds himself able to make it for two weeks without masturbating, why not extend it for another two weeks? It is my experience that most habits will be effectively broken if the overcomer is able to extend the challenge for six to eight weeks.

Every temptation that has come your way is the kind that normally comes to people. For God keeps His promise, and He will not allow you to be tempted beyond your power to resist; but at the time you are tempted He will give you the power to endure it, and so provide you with a way out (see 1 Cor. 10:13).

Seven Relational Changes

In addition to the seven external, personal changes, there are seven external relationship changes that your overcomer can begin to work on almost immediately. Instruct him in this way:

Begin to sever all homosexual and gay relationships, involvements, romances, emotional dependencies and attachments. I realize that this is not easily done, when, for instance, you have been sharing the mutual expenses of an apartment or when you have very few other people in your life.

Sometimes an overcomer has feelings of affection and love which are very strong and real. These can be almost devastating to bring to an end. It is painful. Yet, I also know that unless you take the steps to end these relationships, you have not really surrendered your healing to the Lord in a wholehearted way. I have heard a hundred rationalizations for not ending these relationships. You may have some of your own. I encourage you to end the self-deception and begin bringing these relationships to a close.

As you begin to end these relationships, it is a good time to repent of the sinful lifestyle you were in. Get before the Lord in prayer. Ask Him to forgive you for each and every sin you committed in these relationships. Recall and name each person that you have sinned with (to the extent that you know them by name), and ask the Lord to break the spiritual and emotional bonds (bondages) you formed by your sexual sins. Ask the Lord to release each person and that you also be released from the memories and spiritual intimacies you formed with these people. Ask the Lord to remove Satan's clutch on your emotional life and deliver you from desiring these evil ways again.

Have you failed to invest quality time in your other relationships with parents, siblings, peers, spouse, your children, or other relatives? Begin to improve these relationships, even if they have been ones of conflict and difficulty. To do nothing is to leave a major area of life unfinished and vulnerable. Tell the Lord that you want to change these troublesome relationships. He will start to show you how. He will open the doors to improving these relationships if He knows that you really desire to do so.

Do you have some good Christian same-sex relationships? These relationships are most important as you redevelop a network of nonsexual, nondependency relationships with others and seek to feel accepted by "straight" males. You might even begin to engage in some manageable male athletic activities. These experiences could make you feel as if you belong and increase feelings of self-acceptance among males as a male.

I also recommend that you find an older, same-sex person to be a special friend. This person should be someone in whom you can confide; who will encourage and support you, and one to whom you can be accountable on a regular basis. Often, this person can be found at the church in which you fellowship.

I recommend that you begin to socialize and enjoy the

company of the opposite sex. I don't recommend that you quickly become involved in an exclusive heterosocial relationship, unless such a relationship is genuinely developing. Your singles group at church may be the place for this. Also, without being sinful, I would encourage you to take notice when you may feel heterosexual feelings, interests, and attractions. Be open to experiencing these without it becoming erotic indulgence. Heterosexual feelings and desires will normally begin to emerge as you start to experience the healing of the Holy Spirit.

Join a support ministry for overcomers. These ministries provide good educational, social, spiritual, and supportive peer relationships. If you are unaware of such a local ministry, write to EXODUS International, P.O. Box 2121, San Rafael, California 94912.

Lastly, consider the benefits of good professional Christian counseling. A good same-sex counselor is recommended. This person will give you a positive, caring, helping relationship; wise counsel, encouragement, and insight. He will enable you to experience and enact the internal healing approach which makes up the focus of the rest of this book. In addition, he will help you draw on your relationship with the Lord as a source of strength and healing.

FOR THE COUNSELOR

There are numerous strategies suggested in this chapter which have proven effective in changing homosexual habits and behaviors. The fact is, your overcomer is going to have to get down to the "nitty-gritty" hard work of breaking habits and addictions which he has reinforced and repeated for a number of years. There is just no other way than to slug it out with himself. This will not last forever, but he will probably have to work at it for some time before he really sees himself changing. Encourage your overcomer with this passage.

In Haggai 2:19, the Lord says, "From this day on I will bless you." Here is the way which C.H. Spurgeon explains this text:

> There had been failure of crops, blasting, and mildew, and all because of the people's sin. Now, the

Lord saw these chastened ones commencing to obey His word, and build His temple, and therefore He says, "From this day . . . when the foundation of the Lord's temple was laid . . . from this day on, I will bless you." If we have lived in any sin and the Spirit leads us to purge ourselves of it, we may reckon upon the blessing of the Lord. His smile, His Spirit, His grace, His fuller revelation of His truth will all prove to us an enlarged blessing. We may fall into greater opposition from man because of our faithfulness, but we shall rise to closer dealings with the Lord our God, and a clearer sight of our acceptance in Him.[1]

Your overcomer will surely begin to receive one blessing upon another when he makes these efforts to obey the Lord and overcome his homosexual habits and behaviors.

Refer to the stress-relief cycle often. It is a helpful conceptual tool for his understanding of what is taking place when he is feeling vulnerable and empty. Help him to follow through on the seven personal and seven relationship change areas. Monitor the way he is making progress and effort in each of these. Most importantly, remind him that a slip, or even a fall, does not put him all the way back to point "0." Rather, progress in this area is more like taking three steps forward and two steps backward. All forward movement is cumulative and makes a difference.

1. C.H. Spurgeon, *The Cheque Book of the Bank of Faith: Being Precious Promises Arranged for Daily Use, with Brief Experimental Comments.* (New York: A.C. Armstrong and Co., 1892), 324.

CHAPTER SIX

IT BEGINS TO HURT— YOU BEGIN TO HEAL

"My father was always right," Jeff said. "He thought he was the only person in our family who had the truth. Everyone else had to agree with him or they never heard the end of it. That's the way I remember him.

"I'll never forget how he would make me stand next to him and force me to listen to him in silence until he was finished saying what he wanted to say. If I disagreed or tried to make him see it differently, he would always talk right over me until I had to stop talking altogether. He always had to win, and of course, I would always lose.

"I would have to stand there in complete frustration and defeat; trapped and victimized. I abandoned all attempts to convince him; feeling anger, hatred, and complete discouragement. Tears would be streaming down my cheeks; I would sob with helplessness, but I wasn't allowed to move until his tirade was over. I would tell him to hit me. That would feel better than his endless verbal whippings. But he went on and on, forcing me to say I agreed with every point he made."

What effect do you think this kind of experience had on Jeff? How did it set him up for homosexuality? What do you think was happening inside of Jeff?

Deep within, Jeff began to bury his feelings of hate, guilt, anger, and shame. He longed for acceptance, but received rejection; he desired closeness, but felt fear; he felt love, yet wanted to hurt and seek revenge.

These emotional imprints caused Jeff to not only reject his real father, but also his inner father. Silently inside, Jeff hardened his heart and refused to form a love bond with his father within. This left him divided and split-off from himself. This broken love bond within left Jeff with Gender Emptiness and an obsessive and compulsive need to find an accepting and loving male who might heal this complex of deprived feelings and pain, so that Jeff could be at one with himself.

What is at the heart of the healing of homosexuality? Homosexuality has very little to do with sex. The sexual involvement with another same-sex person is a symptom; a result; a compromise for the need to be accepted and loved. Healing is emotional work. It is to experience anew, as an adult, the closeness and oneness which was not given from the first father-male in a child's life. It is the healing of that emotional complex of feelings which was left wounded and sensitive from earliest childhood. It is a need to fill that deep sense of being deprived of the love of that first male parent. It is the need to repair the love-bond between the inner child of sensitive and wounded feelings and the inner parent voice which still speaks of rejection, unacceptance, criticism, and denial of worthiness and love.

In order to begin the work of healing this deprivation complex, it would be helpful to have a visual representation of the way in which the personality is constructed. Such a picture will assist you and your overcomer in understanding how the Holy Spirit works within his personality through his mature inner adult voice to heal his whole personality. Scripture says, "Do not conform any longer to the pattern of this world, but be transformed by the renewing of your mind" (Rom. 12:2).

The wholeness and healing which God is working in your overcomer will be done through the transforming of his mind; especially through the inner adult self. All inner healing takes place as the mind begins to effect new ways of thinking, feeling, and acting. The Word says, "Let this mind be in you which was also in Christ Jesus" (Phil. 2:5, KJV).

In this chapter, your overcomer will learn about the conflict and division which exists in his personality; about the way the Holy Spirit works in his unconscious; about his wounded area and the fifteen wounded emotions (needles) and the three inner conversations which produce deep inner healing.

A HOUSE DIVIDED AGAINST ITSELF

One day when Jesus was casting out evil spirits, His enemies accused Him of doing it through the power of Satan. His response to them made famous two basic principles which apply to the inner healing of homosexuality. First, He used an analogy of a house and said, "a house divided against itself will fall" (Luke 11:17). Second, He taught that all things which are empty must be filled with something, whether good or evil. Here, He was teaching that all things abhor a vacuum (Luke 11:25-26).

For a long time, you have been a house divided. Emotionally, it is difficult for a person to be secure if he is divided within. As a person, you have been in conflict with yourself. Your inner child and your inner parent voices have been in conflict within, making you a divided personality. Likewise, because you were not filled with the love of your same-sex parent, a vacuum was left within you. Since nature abhors a vacuum, it began to be filled with those wounded emotions which make up the deprivation complex. "And the final condition of that man is worse than the first," said Jesus (Luke 11:26).

Think of a person as a house (see diagram #1). The material structure of the house—the framing, foundations, windows, doors, walls, floors—represents your body with its five senses. The house, your body, is a container; a bearer of your soul and human spirit. The Bible teaches that a person is body, soul, and human spirit (see 1 Thes. 5:23). Man is a spiritual being; a spirit being who has a soul (personality) and lives in a material body. He is a trinity in unity. It is through your body and its senses that you make contact with the world around you.

Think of your soul as your self or personality. In the house analogy, it is that visible part above ground. Your personality also has a less visible aspect, the human spirit, just as the house has an invisible basement below ground. It is here where Larry's early needs for security and acceptance formed the emotional problem leading to homosexuality.

Diagram 1

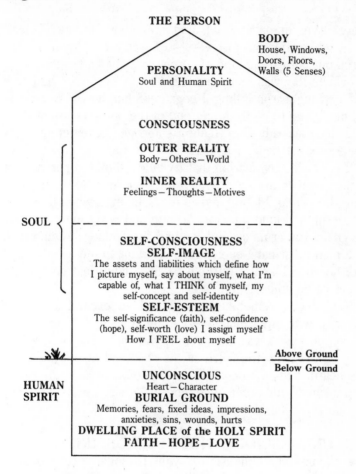

THE PERSON

BODY
House, Windows,
Doors, Floors,
Walls (5 Senses)

PERSONALITY
Soul and Human Spirit

CONSCIOUSNESS

OUTER REALITY
Body—Others—World

INNER REALITY
Feelings—Thoughts—Motives

SOUL

SELF-CONSCIOUSNESS
SELF-IMAGE
The assets and liabilities which define how
I picture myself, say about myself, what I'm
capable of, what I THINK of myself, my
self-concept and self-identity
SELF-ESTEEM
The self-significance (faith), self-confidence
(hope), self-worth (love) I assign myself
How I FEEL about myself

Above Ground
Below Ground

HUMAN
SPIRIT

UNCONSCIOUS
Heart—Character
BURIAL GROUND
Memories, fears, fixed ideas, impressions,
anxieties, sins, wounds, hurts
DWELLING PLACE of the HOLY SPIRIT
FAITH—HOPE—LOVE

"I was about five or six years old," Larry said. "It was probably my first Italian wedding. All the relatives were there. Everyone was loud, and most were drunk. I don't know where my parents were so I was on my own. I wandered out onto some kind of porch which had a ten-foot drop. My Uncle Ray was there and some of my cousins. The porch had a wrought iron railing. I began climbing in and out of the railing, trying to go from one end of the porch to the other. I must have already been feeling some gender emptiness because of what happened next.

"My Uncle Ray, fearing that I would fall off the porch, kept coming over to me and bringing me back near his chair, away from the railing. I found myself really liking it when he would lift me up and hold me close to him and bring me back near his chair. His arms around me and the feeling of being held by a man must have been very important to me even at that age, because I kept returning to the railing just so that he would come and get me.

"I distinctly remember that I had an excited feeling of intimacy with my Uncle Ray. It must have felt somewhat sexual, because I was intrigued by the curly, black chest hair hanging out from the collar of his shirt and his dark masculine beard. I think I began to associate being close to a man with security and acceptance, especially since my own father was so rejecting and remote."

THE UNCONSCIOUS: THE HUMAN SPIRIT

The unconscious dimension of your personality (the level of the house below ground) is your human spirit. The human spirit is the heart or character of your personality. It is the burial ground of the personality. It is also the dwelling place of the Holy Spirit for those who are spiritually reborn. "The Spirit Himself testifies with our spirit that we are God's children" (Rom. 8:16). See also what Jesus Himself says,

> It is what comes out of a man that makes him unclean. . . . For, from within, out of men's hearts come evil thoughts, sexual immorality, theft, murder, adultery, greed, malice, deceit, lewdness, envy, slander, arrogance, and folly (Mark 7:15, 21-22).

Jesus says that it is what comes from deep within a person's heart (the unconscious burial ground) that makes him corrupt, unwhole, and broken. Out of the unconscious come the wounded emotions, sins, and fixed perceptions from the past.

The wonderful news is that once the Holy Spirit is present in your personality, a complete renewal of your whole inner life begins to take place. All the wounds and hurts of the past which have been buried, begin to surface and heal. The Holy Spirit begins to bring wholeness to the personality, and your divided self is being united and integrated.

The emotional wounds which lead to homosexual sinfulness are buried in the unconscious, and it is just these wounded emotions in you which set you up for sin.

The Holy Spirit teaches us in the Bible that "those who live according to the sinful nature have their minds set on what that nature desires; but those who live in accordance to the Spirit have their minds set on what the Spirit desires" (Rom. 8:5). Your mind has been set on your sinful nature's inclination toward homosexual sinning because your mind is still not yet transformed by the Holy Spirit.

Jeremy knows this is true. He knows that his wounded emotional life sets him up for a fall. "I can see how it all came about. My paycheck was held back for some technical reason. This meant that I couldn't pay for the work I had done on the car. Without my car I felt trapped in the house, and here it is, Christmas Day and I'm stuck at home.

"I know that I was feeling those same old feelings all over again. I could hear myself saying, 'Nobody cares about me; I'm just ignored and disregarded again. Even God doesn't come through for me. I'm always a victim.' Before long I was overwhelmed with self-pity and on my way out to a gay bar."

PERSONALITY ANATOMY

When you were a child, you took an inner parent voice into your unconscious burial ground. This voice continues to speak to you within. You hear it but seldom realize that it is a parenting voice from the past. These messages from your inner parent continue to influence you. For you, an overcomer, that inner parent voice often speaks negative and troublesome messages (see diagram #2).

Diagram 2

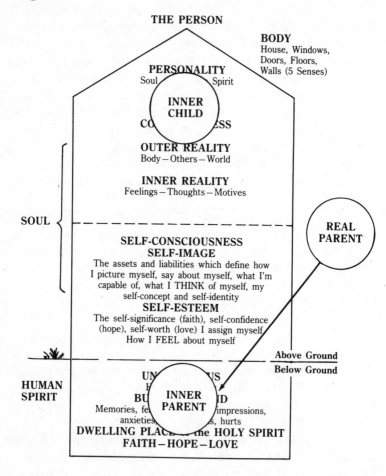

As you left childhood and became an adult, you also left behind a sensitive inner child of feelings from the past which remains entangled and in conflict with your inner parent. Because your relationship with your real parents was troublesome for you in one way or another, your sensitive inner child and critical inner parent are still enmeshed in a troublesome emotional relationship. This has become a wounded area in your unconscious burial ground. It makes up a complex of deprived and wounded feelings (see diagram #3).

Because there was a barrier between you and your real same-sex parent, that inner wall still remains within. This wall keeps your inner child from being loved and accepted by that inner parent part of yourself. You are emotionally divided from an important part of yourself; a part which identifies you with the same sex; a love bond which forms a sense of your identity as a male.

Since you are split off from the same-sex, inner parent part of yourself, you seek to repair (literally, to make a pair) your GE by forming a love bond with another same sex person. This becomes your emotional obsession.

THE WOUNDED AREA: A CLOSE-UP
Anyone who grows up in a dysfunctional family or troubled parent-child relationship, develops an area of woundedness which I call the deprivation complex: one of interacting sensitive feelings which together create a deprived and empty condition.

What does this wounded area look like? (see diagram #4) First, since it is a wounded area of your personality, it is not easily visible to you. Rather, it is hidden, and you are often unaware of it. It is so much a part of your ordinary way of thinking and feeling that it is hard for you to see it for what it really is. Second, you will resist paying attention to it even when you become aware of it because it is sensitive and painful.

NEEDLES
This wounded area is composed of a number of very sensitive and troublesome emotions which I call needles. These troublesome and sensitive feelings originate from those childhood

Diagram 3

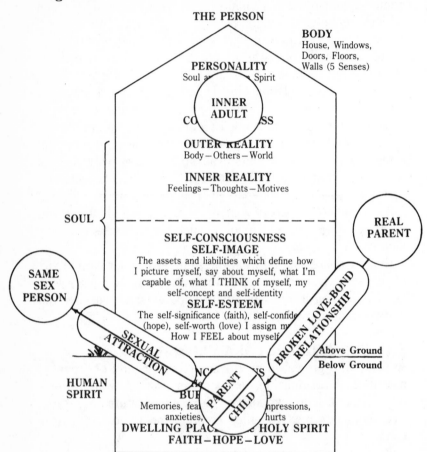

THE PERSON

BODY
House, Windows,
Doors, Floors,
Walls (5 Senses)

PERSONALITY
Soul a   Spirit

INNER
ADULT

CO   SS

OUTER REALITY
Body — Others — World

INNER REALITY
Feelings — Thoughts — Motives

SOUL {

SELF-CONSCIOUSNESS
SELF-IMAGE
The assets and liabilities which define how
I picture myself, say about myself, what I'm
capable of, what I THINK of myself, my
self-concept and self-identity
SELF-ESTEEM
The self-significance (faith), self-confide
(hope), self-worth (love) I assign m
How I FEEL about mysel

REAL
PARENT

SAME
SEX
PERSON

BROKEN LOVE-BOND
RELATIONSHIP

SEXUAL
ATTRACTION

Above Ground
Below Ground

HUMAN
SPIRIT

NC   S
BU   D
Memories, fea   npressions,
anxieties,   hurts
DWELLING PLAC   HOLY SPIRIT
FAITH — HOPE — LOVE

PARENT

CHILD

DIAGRAM 4

Close-Up of Wounded Area and Fifteen Needles

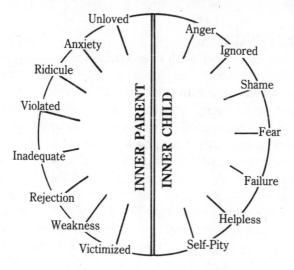

experiences with your parents, siblings, peers, teachers, pastors, and others. They are like sharp needles which continue to stab you with jolts of pain whenever they are experienced. They keep that wounded area alive and charged with pain and hurt.

These wounded emotions make up the deprivation complex which keeps homosexuality alive because they keep you emotionally unhealed. As long as you remain unhealed, you feel that obsessive need to form a love bond with another male. You can see that healing these troublesome feelings is at the heart of the recovery process.

Danny goes from one relationship to another. The last time I spoke with him, he was in tears. His last relationship broke up and he was seriously considering killing himself. He had developed a strong emotional dependency (ED) and attachment to Ramon. At twenty-four years of age, Danny had been in eight serious relationships with other men. He always found others who seemed to take advantage of him and exploit him. In each of these relationships he would let this happen until the old emotional wounds were stimulated once again. Then he would feel abused and violated, rejected and victimized, overwhelmed and depressed. None of these men, who are empty themselves, ever fill Danny's emotional hunger for acceptance and love.

FIFTEEN NEEDLES

In my therapeutic work with overcomers over several years, I began to take note of the feelings that seem to come up again and again. I began to notice fifteen troubling emotions. Your emotional healing, and the healing of homosexuality, depends to a great degree on your coming to know which of these emotions trouble you, and your willingness to begin dealing with these emotions in more effective ways than you have in the past. As you look at each of these sensitive feelings which make up your deprivation complex, you may recognize that some of them are still *highly charged* (hc) with pain, others are *moderately charged* (mc) with pain, and some are only *slightly charged* (sc) with pain. Place an "hc," "mc," or an "sc" next to each set of feelings. This will help you begin to identify the feelings which will need your primary attention.

Once you have identified the highly charged and moderately charged feelings, begin to monitor them as you go through the next several weeks. Which ones keep coming up again and again? Which ones especially seem to emerge just before you feel homosexually tempted? What incidents provoke them?

In going through these pairs of feelings, you may also recognize that many of these feelings began in the presence of your parents. See if you can begin to connect these feelings with specific people from your past and with incidents (stories) from your past in which these feelings were prominent. I would strongly encourage you to both write out these stories and verbally share them with your special friend or counselor. Both writing them out and verbally telling them will be used by the Holy Spirit to heal the wounded feelings associated with them.

1. **Unloved and worthless.** These twin feelings head the list because feeling unloved and worthless is at the core of the deprivation complex. To feel unloved is to feel unwanted, devalued, unworthwhile. It is a feeling of unimportance and of

being unappreciated and not special to anyone. Every person needs to feel special to someone and to belong to someone in a special way. Feeling unloved and worthless is to harbor a deep, secret doubt about your self-worth and value. It is a sensitive and painful underlying, undermining attack on your self-esteem and self-acceptance.

2. **Anxiety and depression.** Anxiety is a feeling of dread, worry, and apprehension. Do you sometimes feel as if something is weighing on you; some responsibility, care, duty, or unfinished burden? There is a sense of some impending danger or attack that may be coming to you. You sometimes feel as if something worse is about to happen. It is vague and intangible but present nevertheless.

Depression can make you feel purposeless; that you are useless and have no interest in life. You may feel that life is unfair, bleak, and a bitter struggle. You may feel that you are always engaged in battle and always under some kind of burden.

3. **Anger and irritation.** I find that many overcomers have trouble with anger. I often see the "four buddies"— anger, sadness, guilt, and depression—hanging around together. You find it hard to get angry, don't you? When you do, it can be explosive. More often, you hold anger back because angry feelings make you feel guilty and self-rejecting. So you try to avoid anger by covering it up in some way. You repress anger and deny anger, and this leads to guilt, sadness, and depression. Internalized anger is a major destroyer of self-esteem.

4. **Ridicule and humiliation.** You may have been openly ridiculed and criticized by your parents (or others) in private or in front of others. You may have been told that you were stupid, dumb, or made to feel deficient in some way. Now you are needled by any sign of ridicule and humiliation. You are supersensitive to any comment that indicates someone thinks poorly of you. Do you ever find yourself a bit paranoid about what others may be feeling or thinking about you?

5. **Disregarded and ignored.** As a child perhaps you were not openly ridiculed but instead were painfully ignored, neglected, or went unnoticed. The lack of attention left you with a sense that you are not worth noticing, not sought after,

chosen, respected, or wanted. You come to disregard and depreciate yourself. You may consider yourself uninteresting and unenjoyable to be with. You put yourself down and feel unworthy of any attention or affection that comes your way.

Frank notices how important clothes are to him. He spends an exorbitant amount of money on clothes. Why? To be noticed! Many evenings in the past he would get all dressed up just to go to a gay bar and be noticed. It felt so good to get the attention of other men, even if there was no sex.

6. **Violated and abused.** You may have been physically, sexually, or emotionally violated as a child. You may have had parents, siblings, or relatives who terrorized and tyrannized you. This may have left you with an exaggerated fear of attack, violence, physical force, aggressiveness, or bodily harm. You may feel distrusting, self-protective, and fearful of intimacy. You sometimes feel bad or guilty. You are very afraid of physical touch.

Scott warns people not to touch him. He says he doesn't trust people touching him. He doesn't believe he was physically or sexually abused as a child, but he's unsure. Scott recognizes that he has an emotional screen or barrier between himself and all other people. He won't let anyone penetrate it.

In therapy with Scott, I sat directly in front of him. I asked him to make continuous eye contact with me. Then I asked him to close his eyes and imagine that I was approaching him. He said that this caused him great apprehension and anxiety. Gradually, he let me touch his hands with mine. Later, he worked through his fear of being touched and hugged by me.

7. **Guilt and shame.** You may have a strong, nagging feeling of guilt and self-criticism whenever you suspect you have done something wrong. Guilt is the conviction of the Holy Spirit and is to be expected. Shame is not of the Holy Spirit and results from someone always telling you the "shoulds" and the "oughts." This made you emotionally oversensitive and unsure of your adequacy.

If you were shamed as a child, you were made to feel exposed and caught with "wrong" feelings like anger, criticism, or disagreement. This caused you so much pain that you now keep "on guard" so that you don't violate these exaggerated internal standards. This kind of shame is very different from the appropriate guilt or remorse over sin.

8. **Incompetent and inadequate.** Joe finds himself having internal dialogues like these:

Inner Parent (IP) "You sure are stupid. Why did you say that to him?"

Inner Child (IC) "I don't know; it was all I could think of at the time."

(IP) "Well, he's really going to think that you're a jerk. You really should watch what you're saying."

(IC) "I can't help it. Sometimes I just act before I think. I get so nervous that I just want to say whatever comes to mind as quickly as possible."

(IP) "Well, think before you act. Why don't you think first? You're always acting like a fool in front of me. You make me so embarrassed."

(IC) "I'm sorry! I'm sorry! I didn't mean to embarrass you."

(IP) "I can never trust you. You're always doing something wrong. What's the matter with you anyway?"

Does this sound at all familiar? You still carry on those inner parent-child dialogues in which you re-create what you actually heard as a child or thought you heard. The end result is that you feel inadequate, incompetent, deficient, unable, lacking, and disabled in some way.

9. **Fear and fright.** Are you a fearful person? Are you preoccupied with fears? Are there situations, things, or people which cause you fear? Does fear seem to dominate and pervade many of the choices and options you select? Is your life somewhat limited and restricted because fears prevent you from doing certain things? Ralph tries to avoid his female boss most of the time because of her aggressiveness. She can get very loud and nasty at times. She can be sarcastic and rude when she confronts others. Ralph makes it a point to try to always stay on her good side. He fears having a run-in with her, even to the extent of sacrificing some of his own rights and freedom.

Fear has dominated most of Ralph's life. He has always been afraid of sports because he feared getting injured. Because some of his new friends are athletic, he declines invitations from them when they go skiing or climbing. He takes very few risks in life.

10. **Rejection and condemnation.** Many times you feel sensitive to rejection and interpret what others do as signs of rejection toward you. You also can be very condemning in the way you speak to yourself internally.

11. **Failure and defeat.** Many times you have the feeling that you have failed. You feel defeated and unsuccessful. Perhaps you remember trying to do things with your parent which were just not enough to please him. You felt your efforts were in vain. You felt like giving up, and sometimes still say, "What's the use?" Steve would try to help his older brother when he worked on his car. But being sensitive, Steve would become fearful and nervous around his brother. Instead of these experiences making him feel closer to his very masculine brother, they would emphasize Steve's inadequacies.

Once, Steve was being picked on by other boys in the neighborhood. He finally got the courage to go to his brother to ask him for help. His brother began to show him how to fist fight. Steve was terrified to do this. Now he felt like he would let his brother down as well. So instead of challenging the neighborhood kids in a fight, he walked miles out of his way to avoid them after school. When his brother found out about this, it reinforced his self-image as a weakling and a failure.

12. **Weakness and lack of confidence.** In some ways this pair of feelings is a basic underlying condition in all overcomers. You may often sense an impotency; a lack of self-sufficiency and self-reliance. You lack the fortitude, the strength and "guts" to assert yourself; to say no when you have to. You refuse to force yourself through difficult emotional times. You often lack a tolerance for frustration and for times when there is little gratification. You sometimes cannot hold on long enough when you're in pain, and so you run to masturbation, pornography, and sexual acting out.

13. **Helpless and hopeless.** You may have times when you feel completely unable to handle things. You feel like throwing in the towel and giving up. You feel discouraged, despondent, and despairing. You lack a sense of hope and

optimism. Many times, you are impatient and cannot hold on. You feel like there is no light at the end of the tunnel. You don't believe things can ever get better, and if they do, they must be completely and totally better. All or nothing! If you can't have it all, you're hopeless. You tend to think in these black and white ways.

14. **Victimized and oppressed.** Often you succumb to being a victim or thinking like a victimized person. You give up, you give in, and allow others to oppress you and offend you. You don't stand up for yourself and defend yourself. You would rather not make waves. You do not initiate with others enough. You hold back and expect others to take the lead. You are cautious and careful.

15. **Self-pity, sadness, and overwhelmed.** These are big wounded feelings among overcomers. You can spend a lot of private time consoling and commiserating with yourself. You feel sorry for yourself and declare yourself a defeated and overwhelmed person by life and circumstances. The bottom falls out every so often. You cave in inside. You fall apart emotionally. You regress to tears or tantrums. You become absorbed in feeling sad and sorrowful.

YOUR INNER ADULT: CHRIST IN YOU

You have a critical inner parent in you and a very sensitive inner child in you. They are still emotionally enmeshed in painful dialogues in your unconscious. This wounded area is composed of a number of sensitive feelings or needles that make up your deprivation complex.

There is another part of your personality, and it is the strongest part of your personality. It is your inner adult (see diagram #3). Your inner adult is that voice in your personality which should gradually take greater control and direction over your whole personality. Your inner adult is the mature and Spirit-led voice of Christ in you. Your whole personality is now under the direction and power of the Holy Spirit, the Spirit of Christ in you. Your whole personality is being transformed by the renewing of your mind in Christ Jesus. For "God hath not given us the spirit of fear; but of power and of love, and of a sound mind" (2 Tim. 1:7, KJV). The Bible also tells you that you "have not received the spirit of the world but the Spirit who is from God, that we may understand what God has freely given us" (1 Cor. 2:12).

Your inner adult is under the guidance and direction of the mind of Christ. It is through the Holy Spirit in you that God intends to heal your personality and wounded emotions. It is through the Holy Spirit that the wall between your inner child and inner parent will be removed. It is through the Holy Spirit that you will be reconciled and renewed in your troublesome relationships with those from whom you are alienated.

It is by the Holy Spirit that homosexuality will be healed. " 'Not by might, nor by power, but by My Spirit,' saith the Lord of hosts" (Zech. 4:6, KJV).

As you yield to the Holy Spirit in you to take control over your inner life, He will operate through your inner adult voice to heal those critical inner parent messages and that sensitive child in you. Then your inner child will no longer be enmeshed with your critical inner parent and the emotional relationship will be reconciled. You will begin to accept yourself as a person and a man, and you will no longer need to look to other men for gratification and love in sinful ways.

THE HEART OF INNER HEALING: THREE INNER CONVERSATIONS

Three conversations within make up the quality of your overcomer's inner life. They are the heart of his inner healing. They are the three relationships of every Christian person.

The first is the inner conversation with the Lord. The second is the inner dialogue between oneself and the inner parent. The third is the inner dialogue between oneself and the inner child.

The quality of these three inner conversations or dialogues affects the quality of your overcomer's real relationships with God, others, and his Self. Jesus points to these three relationships when He speaks of what is most important in life. He says, " 'Love the Lord your God with all your heart and with all your soul and with all your strength and with all your mind'; and, 'Love your neighbor as you love yourself' " (Luke 10:27).

Jesus is teaching that there is a proper love of self which

affects one's love of God and others. The quality of our life within ourselves greatly affects our relationship to God and to others. Those conversations we have within ourselves affects all of life.

FOR THE COUNSELOR
In this chapter I presented a picture of the personality and introduced the concepts of inner child, inner parent, inner adult, and the wounded area or deprivation complex of wounded emotions. The inner healing of homosexuality takes place as your overcomer begins to engage in those three dialogues under the power of his Spirit-led inner adult. In the next chapter we examine those inner conversations with the Lord.

Review the fifteen needles. These wounded emotions will appear and reappear over and over again in your overcomer. You need to be aware of their pervasive presence. One of the most important and helpful things you can do with your overcomer is to continually point out these needles and help him work through them in the safety of his relationship with you. They appear in each of the three conversations we will be examining in the following chapters.

Pray with your overcomer:

Father, I thank You that You have called me to this journey of healing. I open my heart to You, Father, and ask You to reveal the wounded emotions of my life. Father, help me to really know myself. Let me not be afraid to feel my painful feelings. Jesus, remind me of the stories and experiences of my childhood, so that Your Holy Spirit can bring them into the light where I can see them and where You can heal them. I thank You, Father. I trust You, Jesus. In Your precious and powerful name, I pray these things. Amen.

CHAPTER SEVEN

PUTTING AWAY CHILDISH THINGS: CONVERSATIONS WITH GOD

When a farmer plants corn and it starts to grow, he must carefully cultivate between the rows to remove weeds. Weed seeds that were in the soil before the corn seeds were planted usually sprout faster and grow taller than the corn in the first couple of weeks, drawing upon essential supplies of sunshine, water, and nutrients. The farmer only has to cultivate a few times, because once the cornstalks get going, they take away the essentials from the weeds. The old weeds cannot take over again, and the desirable, healthy plants no longer need any help.[1]

Your overcomer made a decision to change his homosexual disorientation. He wants to change. He even made a number of those external personal and relational changes. Now, the hard work begins. It is the work of replacing old habits with new ones. The weed seeds of homosexual feelings and desires, reinforced by certain behaviors, are already in him.

In the past, he let those weed seeds sprout, and he even cultivated them for a while. If he just cut the weeds down (the external changes), they'll grow up again because the seeds are still there in the burial ground of his heart. It is time to dig out the weed seeds and roots and plant the corn of new habits of feeling and thinking. Once the corn of new internal habits is planted, cultivated, and allowed to grow, it will crowd out and force out the weed seeds of homosexuality.

There are three internal conversations which need changing. One is the way your overcomer dialogues with the Lord. A second is his conversations with his inner parent voice; that voice of criticism, authority, acceptance, dependency, intimacy, and sexual connection which is perceived in people with whom he lives, works, and worships. A third is the conversations he has with his inner child of feelings.

When he has learned to change these three important interior conversations, your overcomer will crowd out and force out the seeds of emotional pain which lead him into homosexual sin. He will also see the corn of heterosexuality and emotional wholeness emerge. This chapter will help you to help your overcomer change the way he speaks with the Lord about his problems and struggles with homosexuality.

When your overcomer changes these three conversations enough, he will become the person he is attracted to because he will have developed those inner characteristics of strength, security, and self-confidence he keeps looking for in others. Then the homosexual struggle will lose its intensity and come to an end.

GROWING IN THE KNOWLEDGE OF GOD

Often, the way he speaks to God is a result of how his sensitive inner child and critical inner parent feel about and see God. So much of his life as an overcomer can be dominated by the reactions and biases of his inner child and parent. He has lived behind a wall, a screen, a filter of shame and self-criticism through which he looks at his relationship with God, himself, and others.

His interior talk with the Lord rarely comes from his rational, mature, Spirit-led inner adult. Since this is so, he may have a false and inaccurate view of God and of the way he thinks God sees him. Because his perception of God is distorted, he frequently feels as if God is unreal, inaccessible, unapproachable, unknowable, judgmental, and punitive.

He may often find himself speaking to God out of fear and guilt, assuming that God despises him and has rejected him.

Notice therefore that he relates to God and converses with God through the filters of those wounded needles which make up that painful, inner parent-child conflict.

A.W. Tozer says,

> It is impossible to keep our moral practices sound and our inward attitudes right while our idea of God is erroneous or inadequate. A right conception of God is basic . . . to practical Christian living. It is to worship what the foundation is to the temple; where it is inadequate or out of plumb the whole structure must sooner or later collapse.[2]

Scripture says, "When I was a child, I talked like a child, I thought like a child, I reasoned like a child. When I became a man I put childish things away" (1 Cor. 13:11).

Unless your overcomer engages in accurate communication with God, he will be limiting the grace and support which the Lord desires to bestow on him. Instead, he will be blocking the healing work of the Holy Spirit within him. The Word says, "No eye has seen, no ear has heard, no mind has conceived, what God has prepared for those who love Him — but God has revealed it to us by His Spirit" (1 Cor. 2:9-10).

Remember, your overcomer's healing is under the direction and power of the Holy Spirit. Therefore, he must maintain an open channel between himself and God through the Holy Spirit so that he may receive what God wants him to have. The Holy Spirit will bring him the blessings, guidance, support, and strength he needs to dig up the weed seeds of homosexuality and emotional woundedness, if he yields to the working of the Spirit of Christ in his inner adult self. "The Spirit searches all things, even the deep things of God" (1 Cor. 2:10).

Begin to ask your overcomer these questions: How do you speak and listen to God? Is your conversation with the Lord dominated by your critical inner parent and sensitive inner child? Is your relationship with God frustrating and seemingly fruitless? Do you feel cut off from him and abandoned? Is your relationship with Him distant, numb, and dull? Do you want to experience Him and know Him better? Do you long to know the deep things of God?

In my counseling work with Christians struggling with homosexuality, I have identified at least seven ways that overcomers distort their inner conversations with God. As a result, I believe that they frequently quench and grieve the Holy Spirit. I believe that they block the healing power of God in their life by these inaccurate ways of dialoguing with God.

See if your overcomer's conversations with God are infected by these false attitudes of his critical inner parent and sensitive inner child. I believe that if he can begin to correct these false ways of speaking with God, he will see a new and tremendous source of strength and power released in his heart by the Holy Spirit. I have seen this happen over and over again in those I have ministered to, "according to the working of His mighty power" (Eph. 1:19, KJV).

Talk to your overcomer in this way:

1. **God is unconditional love. Therefore, you are accepted, never rejected.** When you speak to God from your burdened and guilty heart after you have fallen into homosexual sin, remember, He never, ever, stops loving you. You are one of His children, brought into His family by your faith in Jesus through the power of the Word and the Holy Spirit.

You are completely acceptable to Him. Yes, you! You, with your erotic temptations; you, with your sexual obsessions; you, with your secret, sensual, vulgar, embarrassing, pornographic fantasies and temptations; you, with your history of bizarre sexual experiences of which you are so ashamed.

He loves you, even if you have committed homosexual sin just one minute ago. He loves you in spite of all this, though He seeks to take you away from all this as well. He loves you, though your sins grieve Him. Listen to His Word:

> I have loved you with an everlasting love. I have
> drawn you with loving-kindness (Jer. 31:3).

and,

> Who will bring any charge against those whom God
> has chosen? It is God who justifies. Who is He that
> condemns? (Rom. 8:33-34)

and,

> There is now no condemnation for those who are
> in Christ Jesus . . . He who did not spare His Son,
> but gave Him up for us all (Rom. 8:1, 32).

God has already accepted Jesus' death as sufficient for all your sins. As a saved person you are securely in God's hands. He never forsakes you or leaves you. His love for us is based on His unchangeable nature; and His nature is love. It is not based on our feelings or our good behavior.

This is hard for Mike to accept. Mike often gets discouraged when he tries to overcome his temptation to watch good-looking men. When he tries different techniques but then gives in, he feels certain God must despise him.

When that jogger went by the other day, he just couldn't take his eyes off of him. He looked like the "perfect specimen of the male species." Strong legs, good build, dark hair, and a handsome face. He got all caught up in watching his body movement as he ran past his house. Finally, he caught himself and turned away. But the memory stayed with him for hours.

Then he began a familiar cycle. He felt guilty for giving in to the temptation. Guilt led to anger at himself. Anger led to self-condemnation, and then to discouragement and depression. These are the familiar "buddies" that hang around together.

He felt evil and sinful, and was sure that God had rejected him. Later, he snapped at his wife and was impatient with his children. A familiar cycle. Mike has been through this many times before. How about you?

What do you do when you find yourself in this cycle? Think about it a minute. Do you let it run its course? Do you try to counteract it in some mature way?

Mike is learning to change his conversation with God during times like this, and it's making a difference. First, he begins to get in touch with his feelings and tolerate them for a while. In the past he would be so uncomfortable with his feelings of shame, guilt, and anger, that he would quickly deny and repress them. Now, he doesn't run from them.

Mike uses the Word to counteract the cycle. He uses one of the verses cited earlier, or this one, "In all creation [there is nothing that will] separate us from the love of God that is in Christ Jesus our Lord" (Rom. 8:39).

He is learning to break the familiar cycle of lust, indulgence, self-condemnation, discouragement, depression, and hopelessness. I call this the SATAN CYCLE. The devil has victory over you if he can get you to feel hopeless and discouraged. In this warfare in overcoming homosexuality, hopelessness and discouragement are Satan's great weapons.

Mike breaks this cycle by being in touch with his feelings and not running from them, and by calling on the power of the Holy Spirit in the Word of God. When he confesses his sin and repents and believes the Word, he is reminded of God's enduring, never-changing, unconditional love for him.

2. God is spirit. Therefore, worship Him, don't work for Him. Many overcomers have an underlying attitude that they must work for God to prove themselves acceptable to Him. But the Lord doesn't need or want your good works as evidence of your acceptability to Him. If your works are good, it is because they come from your heart. The Lord looks upon the heart.

God is looking for those true worshipers in Spirit and in truth (John 4:23), for God is Spirit (v. 24).

Mitch was at work when a male customer came to his clothing department. The man was dressed in a bright-colored shirt which flattered his broad shoulders and tanned face. His blond hair and white teeth caught Mitch's attention immediately. Quickly Mitch caught himself and began relating to the customer in a stiff, indifferent matter-of-fact sort of way. He made little eye contact with him and pretended that he was distracted.

Later, he was pleased with himself and felt sure that God was also. After all, he didn't take advantage of the situation. He avoided indulging his attraction to this customer.

It is true, Mitch effectively resisted this temptation. At the same time though, Mitch was engaging in a sort of "score-keeping" mentality with God. At the end of the day, if he has overcome temptations, he believes himself acceptable to God. On the other hand, if he counts up a number of failures, then he feels cut off and remote from God. God, he realizes, has become a taskmaster; a record keeper of his successes and failures.

Mitch also realizes that this was the same way he was treated by his parents. He had to work to prove that he was acceptable to them. At the same time, he felt a growing resentment underneath. Their love for him was always conditional. This same work ethic carries over in relationships to others and to God. He can never let up. He must always be responsible and productive. He must constantly be doing things for others. He has a workaholic mentality.

But God is Spirit. He seeks spiritual responses of a heart that is grateful, thankful, faithful, hope filled, and loving. He seeks a worship that is truthful and real. He may love your efforts, but He loves you more. You don't need to work to be acceptable to Him. If you wish to do for God, the doing flows from a loving and grateful heart.

This is a difficult mental attitude to change for Mitch. Instead of counting his successes or failures with temptation, he is learning to bring whatever he experiences to the Lord in truthfulness. If he has been successful, he comes to the Lord in thanksgiving. If he has failed, he comes to the Lord in confession, repentance, and honesty. He continues to trust and believe that he is accepted. As the old hymn says,

> Just as I am, without one plea,
> But that Thy blood was shed for me.
> And that Thou bidst me come to Thee,
> O Lamb of God, I come, I come.

This more real and truthful attitude with God has helped Mitch be more open and honest in other relationships and in his own emotional life as well. He can see how this is changing his own self-acceptance and he is feeling more whole and healed.

3. **God is omniscient. Therefore, reveal, don't conceal.** A real relationship with God is characterized by absolute truthfulness. Honesty with God is always a powerful source of healing. God knows all things about you. There is nothing to hide from Him. Reflect on this reality for a moment. He knows your sin. He knows your double-mindedness; your masks; your secret life of vulgarity and eroticism. He knows all.

> Nothing in all creation is hidden from God's sight. Everything is uncovered and laid bare before the eyes of Him to whom we must give account (Heb. 4:13).

You should take the Psalm 139 position which says, "O Lord, You have searched me and You know me.... Where can I go from Your Spirit? Where can I flee from Your presence?" (vv. 1, 7)

It is an attitude which says, "Here I am, Lord. You know me completely. There is nothing which I can hide from You. You know all about me. I will bring everything before You. I won't pretend to conceal anything. Whatever it is that I am struggling with—no matter how vile or vulgar or vain—I bring it to You in the plain and uncovered truth."

Fred tries to conceal rather than reveal to God. He tries to hide his failures and temptations from God. It is all a part of Fred's obsessive-compulsive personality.

Many Christians, like Fred, who struggle with homosexuality are obsessive-compulsive in their personality functioning. Fred tries to maintain a life of extraordinary consistency and rigidity. He places a number of restrictions and restraints on himself. Most of these are like straitjackets in order to control unwanted feelings of anger and resentment.

Fred is very moralistic and legalistic and tends toward self-righteousness. He is meticulous about his daily routines and gets lost in perfectionistic minutiae. All of this serves to keep a tight control over his repressed feelings. Fred lives the form and not the substance of life. It is the letter that is important to him and not the spirit. He is grim, austere, and cheerless. Since he lives by the rule that he must not let God or others down, he must hide all failures and imperfections from God, himself, and others.

An example of Fred's compulsive personality is with masturbation. He has developed a rigid routine whenever he is tempted to masturbate. He starts singing "Amazing Grace" to himself as his first line of defense. If all four verses have not defeated the temptation, he begins to repeat the "Lord's Prayer" over and over again as his second line of defense. Sometimes this works, sometimes it doesn't. Whether it works or not, the emotional and mental cost is very high. Fred has become emotionally rigid and stiff. His whole mentality has become cautious, scrupulous, and perfectionistic. His relationships with others are dull and stale. Fred is no fun to be around. He can't laugh, enjoy himself or life.

He has a view of God that denies God's omniscience. If he could accept an all-knowing God, he would stop playing hide-and-seek with Him. He would be forced to face God in honesty and openness. He would stop hiding his temptations and failures. If he stopped hiding from God, he might stop hiding from himself. If he stopped hiding from himself, he would be more available to others and his relationships would improve.

Knowing that God is omniscient may threaten you or frighten you. At the same time, it should be a great comfort because it means that God knows all about homosexuality and its development in your life. It also means God knows how to heal it.

God knows your struggles and afflictions. He knows the intensity of your pain and anguish over homosexuality. He knows, and His knowing is caring. Let Him know so that He can care for you. Reveal, don't conceal!

4. **God is omnipotent. Therefore, rest, don't test the Lord.** Do you really believe that God is in charge of your life and your healing? Are you constantly questioning Him and testing Him? God says to you,

> Then the word of the Lord came to Jeremiah: "I am the Lord, the God of all mankind. Is there anything too hard for Me?" (Jer. 32:27)

Do you really trust God? Trust is a very important factor in your recovery as well as in your relationship with God and others. Trust is very similar to hope. When you read the passage above and substitute your name for Jeremiah, hearing the omnipotent God of heaven and earth saying this to you personally, doesn't this create a hope and trust in you?

Marty has a hard time trusting in and relying on God's power. Marty doesn't like to depend on anyone. To be dependent means to be weak and inferior. To lean on another person or God is to expose himself to betrayal. He will not let himself become vulnerable ever again. He made this secret vow after his parents betrayed his trust as a child.

This same distrusting attitude pervades all his relationships. He is suspicious of other people's motives and is oversensitive to signs of trickery and deception. He has learned that it is safer to keep an emotional distance from others; to remain strong and independent; to keep a protective wall around his emotional life. This way he can't get hurt again. He has effectively desensitized himself to tender and affectionate feelings. Even his homosexual relationships have been riddled with suspicion and caution. One-night encounters are all that he can tolerate. If the other person is looking for a deeper relationship, Marty pulls away quickly.

Marty gets angry with God. He feels exploited and distrustful of God. He feels like God lets him down a lot. His last fall is an example.

Marty woke up from a nap last Friday night and felt a tremendous urge to be with a man sexually. In the semiconscious state of half sleep, he quickly got dressed and headed for a gay bar and cruising area. He impulsively gets involved with gays because he has such ambivalence about getting intimate and close to people. He has to do it quickly and without much forethought.

He knew what he was doing was wrong, but he wasn't going to let himself stop. He had to be with someone. There was that promise of relief and enjoyment in an otherwise controlled and rigid lifestyle. He just wanted his way. His inner child was feeling lonely and needed closeness and intimacy with someone. It had to be physical, biological, and sexual; not emotional or relational. It had to be quick, not enduring. He could sense there was an underlying defiance and anger toward something or someone in his homosexual sinning. It felt like it was an anger at God.

Before long he met someone. It was an easy pickup. Soon it was over. Then the tears came. He wasn't any more satisfied than when it all started. The expectation of something wonderful happening was always greater than the result. Now he was lonelier than ever. He still didn't belong to anyone. He still didn't feel special to anyone. The encounter left him even more distrustful and angry.

He was angry at life and God. "Why does this happen? Why am I so weak? Why did You curse me with this problem? Why can't You help me, God? Why can't You stop me?"

Marty went home with anger, remorse, and self-pity. The next day a bitterness came over him. He was sulking and irritable. He refused to pray or even think about God. When Sunday came, he refused to go to church.

Marty's big problem is in the way he views God. He refuses to trust in God's love and omnipotence. He refuses to be dependent on God. He tries to rely on his own sufficiency while God is trying to teach him his dependency. He cannot look to God for strength and power. He tried that with his own father and felt betrayed. Over and over again, Marty goes back and forth between wanting to feel independent and autonomous and needing closeness, strength, and affection from others and God. He goes up and down with God, needing Him and refusing to rely on Him.

What about you? Do you see some of these same dynamics operating in your relationship to God? Do you have a hard time really relying on and trusting Him? Is God's omnipotence real to you? When you're under temptation, do you turn to God in real trust and dependency? Do you keep your eyes on Jesus? Don't test Him; rest in Him!

Say to the Lord, "I will take refuge in the shadow of Your wings until the disaster has passed" (Ps. 57:1), and "My grace is sufficient for you, for My power is made perfect in your weakness" (2 Cor. 12:9).

5. **God is holy and good. Therefore, expect, don't neglect.** Because God's nature is holiness and goodness, you can expect the best from Him continuously. Do you believe that? Don't neglect what He is providing for you, and what He is putting in your very path. In everything, but especially in those difficult times of trial and temptation, ask:

"What are You giving me?"

"What are You showing me?"

"What do You want of me, Lord?"

Gary is on the road a lot, making deliveries for his company. Rest stops on the highway are often troublesome for him because he frequently encounters gay men there.

Recently, at one such stop, he met Ron who started to

"come on" to him. But Ron seemed hesitant and unsure.

He invited Gary into his car and continued talking with him without making any sexual moves. Several times Gary could hear the urgings of the Holy Spirit to witness to Ron. Gary was ambivalent. Should he make a move on Ron or witness to him?

Then Ron started to talk about life and that he had recently become a new Christian. He asked Gary if he thought that what they were doing was wrong. Did Gary believe he could stop or change? Gary began to tell Ron about the ministry for ex-gays that he attended. Gary also admitted that he was a Christian and said that he knew something was different about Ron. He told Ron that God had been speaking to his heart about witnessing to him. They both started to become tearful as they talked about God's love for them and realized that God had saved them both from sinning.

Ron told Gary that this was the first time that he had come to a rest stop to cruise someone. Gary invited Ron to the next meeting of the ministry. Ron came and was overwhelmed that God had intervened in this strange way to bring him to a ministry where he could get help with his homosexual problem.

The Lord is continuously showing His loving-kindness and goodness. Do you see it? Are you looking for it? Do you expect it, even in the most unlikely places and ways? Are you neglecting it? "Today, if you hear His voice, harden not your hearts" (Ps. 95:7).

6. **God is all truth and justice. Therefore, repent, don't invent excuses.** Dwight left the ex-gay group that night more depressed than when he came. The talk had been heavy and not very uplifting. He had had a bad week. He had just started to try dating women, and the date he had for Saturday just backed out on him. He had another argument with his mother. All the bills seemed due that week, and he wasn't sure if he would be able to keep up his payments on everything. Several times this week he felt like cruising. He had spent a lot of time watching television. He was bored, lonely, tense, and stressed. He didn't just want to go home. He was sick of his apartment. He wanted some action, some fun, some excitement.

He had masturbated a lot this week and indulged in homosexual fantasies freely. He was disgusted with himself. Wrestling on television was becoming his pornographic prelude to masturbation. He was tired of the vicarious sex. He needed someone to be with. He wanted someone to notice him. He wanted to be wanted; and so, after circling the familiar cruising area a few times, he found someone. It was over quickly and he went home depressed.

Dwight is very passive-aggressive. He is always in emotional turmoil. He lacks self-discipline. He often feels cheated and unappreciated. Nothing ever seems to work out for him. He has come to not expect things to improve. He is pessimistic and negativistic.

As a child he received inconsistent treatment from his parents. One minute his mother was over affectionate, the next she was remote and cool toward him. His father was the same way. He vacillated between wanting a great deal of involvement with Dwight which satisfied his father's needs, to long periods when he would not even recognize that Dwight existed. As a result of this treatment, Dwight learned a pattern of quickly shifting moods. He often feels very contentious, intolerant of anything which frustrates him, and unpredictable in his feelings.

After his anonymous sexual encounter, he rationalized it away. He always invents excuses for his behavior. He did this with his parents because he never knew what to expect from them. Now he does the same with God. Instead of confessing his sin and failures and repenting, he finds ways to project his failures onto circumstances.

Dwight is beginning to learn that the only way out of spiritual darkness is to go to God in honesty and seek His forgiveness. Repentance is the only way out of such a situation. Scripture says, "If we confess our sins, He is faithful and just and will forgive us our sins and purify us from all unrighteousness" (1 John 1:9).

You know that you have a secret life of sin and failure. God knows and sees them. They are sins. You must not deny that they are sins. They certainly have emotional underpinnings; nevertheless, they are sinful behaviors. This is why you must make it a regular, if not daily, practice of examining your conscience before the Lord and confessing honestly whatever sins you have committed. He is faithful and just to forgive you.

7. **God is faithful. Therefore, believe, don't be deceived.** God cannot be other than who He is. He cannot act out of character to who He is; and God is faithful. What He has promised to you and what you have heard Him speak to your heart, will come to pass. "Commit thy way unto the Lord, trust also in Him, and He shall bring it to pass" (Ps. 37:5, KJV).

Scott becomes discouraged because he sees many areas of his life which need changing. He is thirty-five years old, has difficulty dating women, is unhappy at work, strained in his relationships at work and with his roommates, lonely and frequently depressed, addicted to pornography, and unable to avoid sexual attractions.

Meditating on God's faithfulness is very important to him because in the midst of all these difficulties he leans on the experience he had with the Lord when he was saved six years ago. The promise the Lord made to him then has been his strength ever since.

He had been active in the lifestyle for about four years when his last relationship broke up. In despair and grief he went to his first meeting of an ex-gay ministry. That night he met Larry. Larry was terminally ill with AIDS. His heart went out to Larry immediately and soon they became good friends. He had no sexual interest in Larry and they spent much time together.

Soon Larry's health caused him to be confined at home and eventually in the hospital. Scott was one of the last people to spend time with Larry before he died. He never forgets Larry's last words to him. "Scott," he said, "God will heal you of homosexuality as He has me. Just trust Him. He is faithful." Then Larry gave Scott the verse of Scripture which had seen him through his own healing and illness. Scott felt that Larry was bequeathing it to him, and he made it his own. "There hath not failed one word of all His good promise" (1 Kings 8:56, KJV). In his time and in his own way, Scott is seeing these words of God come true in his own life. He knows God is faithful.

FOR THE COUNSELOR

There are three important inner conversations which need to change in order to remove the rocks and boulders of low self-esteem and gender emptiness and produce that inner healing which reduces the homosexual disorientation. Changing these conversations changes thinking and affects the transforming of the mind (Rom. 12:2).

In this chapter we looked at the first of these conversations or interior dialogues; the conversation which your overcomer has with the Lord. Often, that conversation is a distorted one. It is based on false perspectives and knowledge of God. Those perspectives need changing as he comes to know God through His real attributes. God is love, spirit, omniscient, omnipotent, holy and good, truth and justice; God is faithful. As the overcomer comes to know the real God, his inner adult will be strengthened; he will be "strengthened with power through His Spirit in the inner man" (Eph. 3:16, NASB).

Your overcomer needs to know the real God. As he changes this internal dialogue with the Lord, he will begin to dig up those weed seeds of emotional pain and plant the corn of heterosexual recovery. He must put away childish things!

Pray together:

Father, because You are all-loving, You will never reject me. This is the love that I have needed all of my life, and it makes me love You with all my heart, soul, mind, and strength, and to trust You completely.

Father, because You are all-Spirit, You long to give me the deepest spiritual treasures of Your heart. This makes me so grateful and thankful that I can worship You in faith, hope, and love. These are the spiritual things I have sought for all of my life.

Father, because You are all-knowing, You know everything about me. This makes it unnecessary to hide anything from You and to let You know me completely. This is the freedom to be open and honest that I've wanted all my life, and it makes me joy-filled and liberated.

Father, because You are all-powerful, You are in charge of my life, my healing, and my wholeness. I can rest in You and trust in You completely.

Father, because You are all-holiness and all-goodness, I can expect Your constant care and watchfulness over me, and this makes me secure and patient and at peace.

Father, because You are all truth and You are just, I know I must confess my failings and sins before You, and this makes me repentant and eager to please You more.

Father, because You are faithful, I know that every promise that You have spoken to my heart shall come to pass, and this makes the journey out of homosexuality assured.

> Humble yourselves, therefore, under God's mighty hand, that He may lift you up in due time. Cast all your anxiety upon Him for He cares for you. . . . And the God of all grace Himself will restore you and make you strong, firm and steadfast (1 Peter 5:6, 10).

Amen!

1. Dennis L. Gibson, *Vitality Therapy: Techniques for Short-Term Counseling* (Grand Rapids: Baker, 1989), 70.
2. A.W. Tozer, *The Knowledge of the Holy* (New York: Harper and Row, 1961), 2.

CHAPTER EIGHT

CONVERSATIONS WITH THE INNER PARENT

Bill can't say no. His boss loads him down with extra assignments and responsibilities, and Bill can't refuse. With people in authority, Bill is always compliant and agreeable to their face. Later, he seethes with resentment and self-criticism.

People in authority stimulate his inner parent voice; a voice to which he remains submissive and compliant as he did when he was a child. People in authority have a fixed claim on Bill's sensitive inner child. As a child, Bill always wanted to please those in authority (his teachers), because they gave him the approval and affirmation which he didn't receive from his own parents. Now, as an adult, his inner child immediately responds in the same "let me win your respect; let me not displease you" mentality.

This is the kind of dialogue that goes on between his inner parent (IP) and his inner child (IC):

(IP) You had better accept these extra assignments if you want my approval and favoritism.

(IC) Yes, I do want your acceptance and approval, so I'll do whatever you want.

(IP) I know you can handle anything I give you, even if it is more than all the other employees.

(IC) Oh, of course I can, I want to be seen as better than everyone else because then I will have that affirmation and love I need so much. I won't do anything to lose that.

(IP) Good! I wouldn't want you to make me unhappy or to assert yourself with me; remember, I'm in authority over you, and you don't like to be in conflict with anyone, especially your boss. Isn't that right?

(IC) Oh, of course! I need your approval too much to ever disagree with you or refuse your every wish. If you disapproved of me or were upset with me, I would feel very guilty. I can't stand to live with guilt. I have a little; just a very little resentment however, because I have to do more than the other employees.

(IP) How dare you get angry at me! You ungrateful jerk!

(IC) Oh, no, no, no! I didn't mean I was angry. Oh, no! I...I...I... was just expressing an opinion, that's all! I take it back; I'm very sorry I even thought that! (How humiliating this is to me. I feel like a fool. Why am I such a weakling? I always give in to my boss. I really am a jerk.)

What kind of a setup do you think this is for Bill? What does this kind of inner conflict do to Bill's self-image and his self-esteem? How does Bill end up feeling about himself after he has this kind of inner turmoil?

This is just the kind of inner stress and irresolute dilemma inside of Bill that begins to pull down his feelings of self-worth, self-respect, and self-acceptance. Whenever Bill encounters angry or guilty feelings toward other people, especially those in authority, Bill has this kind of turmoil within. When this is intensive, over a period of time, Bill's inner child starts to develop a strong need for someone to love him and take away his pain. This need leads to homosexual encounters.

PEOPLE PROVOKE THE INNER PARENT

Recovery from homosexuality involves external personal and relational changes and inner healing of attitudes, thinking, and feelings. This internal change has to do with the three inner dialogues or conversations your overcomer has with the Lord, with his inner parent, and with his inner child.

In this chapter I want to help your overcomer understand his inner parent voice. That's what Bill is learning to do, and it's making a tremendous difference in the way Bill feels about himself.

His parents (and to some extent, his siblings, peers, relatives, teachers, pastors) were the first significant relationships in life. Whatever they did or didn't do, whatever they said, and the way they acted were the first models for patterns of thinking, feeling, and behaving for all other relationships in life. From them he learned the first patterns of emotional reactions and ways of relating that are now part of his adult life. These patterns are ways of protecting and guarding his sensitive wounded emotions; that deprivation complex of painful feelings.

These patterns have all been programmed into the inner parent part of your overcomer's unconscious and continue to influence the way he perceives and responds to others in his life. Without being conscious of it, he reacts to others in certain repetitive ways, over and over again.

Most of these reactions are totally unknown to him. They happen so rapidly and spontaneously that they are already occurring before he can become conscious of them. Even when he does become aware of them, he finds them very difficult to change because they are so well established as reactional habits.

These relational reactions are often negative, restrictive, inhibiting, dysfunctional, and unrewarding. They do not enhance his self-image and self-esteem, and they continue to keep his wounded area sensitive and unhealed. Therefore, they also contribute to keeping him in need of the homosexual compromise. His emotional reactions to people are major setups for homosexual temptation.

When he becomes aware of them, and works to change them, he will find himself changing within, and feeling more integrated and whole. These habitual ways of perceiving, feeling, and behaving in relation to others, and the internal conversations that result, are called transferences.

TRANSFERENCES

The tendency to habitually perceive and react to others as you did with your parents is called a transference. You transfer to others the relational perceptions which you learned from your parents and other significant people, in order to protect your self-image, your self-esteem, your wounded feelings.

Transferences can be both positive and negative. For the overcomer, many of these patterns are negative. Being in touch with and changing those inner transference conversations between your inner parent and inner child is a major source of inner healing that frees up the homosexual need.

See how Bill is learning to manage that inner conversation between his demanding, critical inner parent and sensitive, needy inner child. He allows the reasonable and Spirit-led inner adult (IA) voice to work within.

(IP) You had better accept these assignments if you want my approval and favoritism.

(IC) Yes, I would like your approval and favoritism; but I am not so needy of them that I will let myself be taken advantage of and abused.

(IP) Tough talk! How will you really feel if I get angry and make you feel guilty?

(IC) Well, I won't like it, but I'm learning to tolerate guilty feelings. Try me! (I'd rather not take on any new assignments right now.)

(IP) OK. You asked for it. (You see, your boss is a bit peeved at you.) He's unhappy with you. You're going to have a hard time living with that, are you not?

(IC) OK. I admit it. It's making me a little uncomfortable when I see my boss unhappy with me. Boy, am I covering up my words. "Unhappy, uncomfortable."

(Inner adult, IA) Come on, Bill, what are you really feeling? (Name the real feelings. Stop covering up your feelings.) OK, I feel a little scared and guilty and anxious because I said no to my boss.

(IP) You know that your boss is really disappointed in you in a big way. He probably will never talk to you again, and you will be miserable from this point on.

(IA to IC) No way, think of all the times you have gone out of your way to be a good employee. Your boss may not be thrilled about you saying no this time, but that's not going to make him hate you. Come on, Bill, be reasonable.

When Bill lets the Holy Spirit intervene and separate the inner parent voice from the inner child feelings, he effectively prevents the old familiar deprivation complex of painful feelings from overwhelming him and leading him into homosexual sin. This is what you must learn to do until it becomes the new habit that digs up the weed seeds of homosexuality.

In order to do this, the first thing you must do is to be able to recognize the transferences that stimulate your critical and dysfunctional inner parent voice.

For instance, you may see it as positive when a woman relates to you in a nurturing and solicitous way. It may give you the same comfort you experienced with your mother, the first significant woman in your life. On the other hand, when it is done in a very dominant and demanding way, it probably causes you to feel unmanly and immature. You may feel threatened and frightened by a woman who needs to depend on you or who demands deep intimacy with you. At other times, you may feel strong and confident in meeting her needs.

Another example of a transference that you may be susceptible to is when a woman is very upset and emotional. This may remind you of your mother when she was upset. At such times, you, as a child, had to comfort her and console her. This might arouse the old anxiety your inner child felt at such times; anxiety because you had to forego childhood needs to meet your mother's needs. This probably made you insecure and fearful.

LOVE AND TRANSFERENCE

One of the very positive uses I make of transference in my therapy work with overcomers is to allow a close and emotionally positive transference to take place with my male clients. When this is openly discussed and worked through, the male client is able to experience, perhaps for the first time, a loving relationship with a male that is nonsexual. This is a powerful source of healing.

To the client in therapy, the therapist is a special person on whom he begins to project real and fantasy-like qualities. Not fully conscious of what he is experiencing, the client starts feeling and acting with his therapist as he might with an all-powerful, all-knowing, wise and good nurturing parent. And so begins a powerful therapeutic transference relationship which is important to therapeutic healing.

In longer term therapy, working directly with the transference is vital to personality and life-changing reconstruction of the inner wounded person. When the therapist points out and talks out the client's transferential feelings and behavior at the very time the client is experiencing them, the old troublesome unfinished fears and anxieties are relived again. The difference this time is that they are relived in the open where they can be examined and explored and worked through within the safety of a trusting relationship. The underlying wounds associated with distrust, betrayal, dependency, self-rejection, anger, guilt, fear of intimacy, and lack of confidence begin to lose their grip.

In my counseling work with Jay, I wrote,

It is not surprising, though it deeply moves the heart, to hear a client like Jay say, "I'll tell you the truth. I feel like giving up all the time, but I can't because of you. You have more hope about all this than I do. Nobody else cares about me like you do." Experiencing love is the heart of this therapy, for God is love (1 John 4:8) and this is God-led therapy. Experiencing love means not only to be given love, but to receive it and let it in deep enough and long enough to let the human spirit heal. Then this love must be exercised and given back, initially to the therapist and to God, gradually to others. There were wonderful signs that all this was happening to Jay.

WATCH THESE SIX TRANSFERENCE REACTIONS

Whenever he finds himself having strong positive or negative feelings and reactions to someone or to some event, you can be sure that a transference is taking place. It means that his inner parent is in operation.

There are six transference patterns which he will see happening in his relationships with others. Each may have positive as well as conflictual aspects to them for his self-esteem, self-confidence, and the healing of his wounded area of painful feelings.

— Control, power, dominance, authority
— Judgment, criticism, appreciation, acceptance
— Gender, sexuality, eroticism

- Superior, inferior responses
- Dependency, independence responses
- Intimacy, closeness, affection responses

Which transferences in the list above do you think Bill was having with his boss? What kinds of transferences are triggers and setups for your overcomer's deprivation complex? Let's look at each of these separately.

1. **Control, power, dominance, authority.** Many overcomers grew up in dysfunctional families which could be described as either violent or authoritarian.

In a violent family there is a lot of screaming, yelling, and fighting. Parents can be cruel, outrageous, inflexible, and tyrannical. Children are slapped, hit, punched, and beaten.

In the authoritarian dysfunctional family, there is a closed family unit that cuts itself off from the community for cultural, political, or religious reasons. Power is abused and a strict and oppressive atmosphere prevails. Parents are often demanding, critical, rigid, and inflexible, with impossibly high standards. The many restrictions and rules leave the children feeling emotionally whipped and abused.

If he grew up in either of these types of families, he may be left with an inner child who feels resentful, suffocated, intimidated, isolated, and submissive. When he is with others who are controlling and authoritarian, he may transfer to them feelings of resentment, antagonism, and anger. He may also be surprised to see himself acting in controlling and authoritarian ways with others. He may be over assertive or aggressive or even the opposite, passive and unable to exercise appropriate authority.

In a therapy session with Roy just before he went home for Christmas, he became angry with me because he sensed I was displeased with his progress in counseling. He was encouraged to express his anger. As he started to do this he diverted his eyes and would not look at me. I asked him to make eye contact with me as he became angry, and he did, through many tears. This was a powerful healing and relearning experience for Roy which had a big payoff when he went home for Christmas.

In this one incident he learned that he could be angry and not have to hide it or feel guilty about it. At home, he experienced anger toward his father, but this time he was able to be angry without feeling guilty. This was a great first step in ending the emotional enmeshment he continued to have with his dad which prevented him from accepting himself as a person and a man.

In another example of transference with issues of authority and power, John often becomes silent when his female supervisor takes a strong stand against some policy or regulation. He feels resentful but never confronts these traits in himself or his supervisor. Instead, he withdraws, sulks, and distances himself from everyone for days at a time.

He knows his reaction is stronger than it need be and assumes his inner parent is making a transference reaction. In order to stop the sulking and self-pity, he begins an adult dialogue with his inner parent and notices that he is less tempted homosexually when he works through his transference.

2. **Judgment, criticism, appreciation, acceptance.** Fred has trouble with one particular coworker named Jim. Jim likes to tease others in sarcastic and sometimes, insulting ways. Fred sees no humor in this kind of joking. He feels humiliated by it, and tries to avoid Jim as much as he can. When there are invitations to lunch or parties by fellow workers, Fred often declines to avoid being insulted by Jim.

Fred is self-critical when he views himself as thin-skinned and sensitive to Jim's remarks. Other people seem to take it so much more lightly. He feels ashamed of himself because he fears any form of criticism, even though it is done in humor. All of these inner child feelings are stirred by an inner parent voice of criticism which still has a razor sharpness. Since this makes Fred feel unmanly and emasculated, it directly contributes to his LSE (low self-esteem) and homosexual temptation.

Many overcomers are highly sensitive to people who are critical or judgmental. On the other hand, they may gravitate to those who show them appreciation, and even feel overly dependent on them.

Bill, you remember, has transference reactions with his boss and others in authority. He also struggles with dependency needs. For instance, he gets hurt if Andy, an older man at church, doesn't come up to him on Sunday and talk with him. He has come to expect special attention from Andy, and when he doesn't get it, he thinks he has done something wrong or that he is really not very interesting. He also feels jealous when Andy shows interest in other young men, and is embarrassed about having such feelings.

3. **Gender, sexuality, eroticism.** Does your overcomer find himself somewhat obsessed with the examination of his masculinity-femininity or gender characteristics? Does he wonder about such things as the pitch of his voice, his handshake, his bodily movements, his clothing and hair, and the size of his physique and muscles?

Do you remember the short questionnaire I gave which asked about identity consolidation? How did he respond to those questions?

I have noticed that many overcomers continue to examine their gender identity characteristics throughout the age period from adolescence through the early to mid-thirties. Many overcomers have a preoccupation with maintaining a youthful identity even well into their forties and fifties. Sometimes it is important for a person to consciously work at changing gestures, postures, voice, and behavior which is effeminate for males or masculine for females.

When Tim is around other men at church he always feels overly self-conscious. He is constantly examining himself to see if he is displaying masculine characteristics when he is with other men. He is always comparing himself with other men. He catches himself imitating Frank, a casual, relaxed, and self-confident man. He realizes that he is transferring onto Frank his own desire to be self-confident, strong, and manly.

When he begins to dialogue with his inner parent about these feelings, he becomes less inhibited and more open; less guarded and more spontaneous. This openness usually pays off in freeing him from self-judgments which are often setups for homosexual acting out.

This is how the inner conversation goes:

(IP) Tim, watch those hands, you look like a fairy!
(IC) I know it, and I better stop crossing my legs like a

woman. I am so unlike these other guys. What a fag I must look like.

(IP) They are all noticing that you don't fit in. You'll never look like a real man!

(IC) Oh, what a queer I am. I'll never be a man. I feel so stupid and out of place among men. I am such a failure; I'm . . .

(IA) Wait a minute! Hold everything! Come on, Timmy! Get hold of yourself now! You know that tearing yourself down like this only makes you more alienated than you're already feeling. Let me remind you of the men who really like you and who like to be with you because you share your feelings so openly. Many men admire you for this; isn't that true?

(IC) Yes, it is! OK. I'm going to stop this self-criticism right now. It doesn't help me at all. I need to accept myself as I am.

Eric has a phobia about looking other guys straight in the eyes. Eye contact is too intimate for him. If the guy is especially good-looking and has nice eyes, he has real problems.

Eric is constantly wondering if men are noticing him in sexual ways. He reads erotic meanings into other men's behavior. For instance, Ray, a fellow employee, often makes steady eye contact with Eric. This is just a habit for Ray because he is straight, and looking steadily into another man's eyes is not uncomfortable for him.

When this happens, however, Eric finds it difficult to concentrate on his work because close eye contact is emotionally and sexually charged for Eric. It suggests an intimacy with Ray which precipitates sexual feelings.

If they stand next to each other at the drafting table, Eric becomes very aware of those times when their bodies might accidentally touch. For Ray, this goes completely unnoticed.

Eric knows he is transferring feelings of desire for closeness and emotional intimacy with a man onto Ray and begins to dialogue with his inner parent about this.

(IP) OK, Eric, I caught you again! You're staring into Ray's eyes as if they are pools of water and you want to jump in. Cut it out; you know you are just indulging your erotic appetite.

(IC) I can't help it. I'm sorry. I'm sorry! Oh, I feel so ashamed; so guilty.

(IP) You're so vulgar and obscene. Ray is just trying to do his job, and there you are, having a porno free-for-all.

(IC) Please stop, I feel bad enough. Why do I do this all the time? I'm obsessed with fantasies about Ray.

(IA) Eric, listen to me a minute. Calm down. Relax a minute. Let me help you think this through. Being with Ray makes you want that closeness which you never had with your dad. That closeness, emotionally speaking is OK, as long as it doesn't get to be sexual.

Since that's very unlikely with Ray, how about trying some things to break the idol. For instance, instead of making your accidental touching a big secretive thing, I want you to purposely touch him in friendliness. Grab his forearm, and say, "Hey, Ray, I really like that idea," or jokingly, "Come on, Ray, you don't really want to do it (referring to your work) that way, do you?" (as you push him on the shoulder). Try it, Eric! Go ahead!

(IC) (Trying it.) Yeah, I see what you mean. Purposely touching Ray takes the seriousness and fantasy out of it. And I notice, it relaxes me with him. I feel more like I'm with a friend than an idol.

Eric has learned to reduce his hyper-sexual responses by opening up his inner dialogues to his inner adult voice.

4. **Superior, inferior responses.** Making transference comparisons with others about feelings of being superior or inferior may be something your overcomer experiences. This is largely related to feelings of low self-esteem, which, as we saw in chapter 4, is at the root of homosexuality.

He may assume he is inferior to someone and automatically relate to others on this assumption. This may lead him to avoid arguments, refrain from asserting himself, being compliant-defiant, never questioning anyone's decisions, being placating, and disregarding others.

When Tom makes an error in his work, he sees himself as a failure. He tries to cover up this feeling of failure by constantly excusing himself and apologizing. As a result, he is very guarded, unrelaxed, and inhibited. He tries to maintain an outward appearance of smiles and pleasantness when underneath he is anxious, irritated, and stressed out.

Tom is always protecting his self-esteem. He often feels so poorly about himself that he lives a double life. On the surface, he is cooperative, kind, gracious, and friendly. Underneath, he is insecure, anxious, cautious, and very unhappy. Scripture wisely tells us that the double-minded man is unstable in all his ways (James 1:8).

Speak to your overcomer in this way:

Since your self-esteem underlies this and other troublesome transference reactions, you may want to look at your own self-esteem and assess how you really feel about yourself.

Remember, self-esteem is the way you feel about yourself; self-image is the way you think about yourself. Improving your self-esteem plays a major role in the recovery from homosexuality since it is the underlying root cause of all personality and emotional problems.

Caution! If the results show a low self-esteem, remember Romans 8:28. Second, any answers which you mark a "4" or "5," should be talked about with your special friend or counselor.

SELF-ESTEEM QUESTIONNAIRE

Use numbers 1 through 5 to rate each of these statements:

1 = Not true at all   2 = Only slightly true   3 = Somewhat true   4 = Mostly true   5 = Very true

1. _____ I am often critical and judgmental of others.
2. _____ I often feel the need to defend myself, at least in my mind.
3. _____ I am frequently irritated and angry, though it may not show.
4. _____ I let others take advantage of me and walk over me.
5. _____ If I were really honest, I'd have to say that I'm

really afraid of closeness and intimacy with people at an emotional level.

6. _____ I keep my emotions bottled up inside a lot.

7. _____ I tend to be a bit compulsive and a perfectionist.

8. _____ I feel overwhelmed many times.

9. _____ My conscience seems to be very sensitive.

10. _____ I can get very pessimistic and gloomy at times.

11. _____ I am not comfortable in telling people that I love or need them.

12. _____ I don't feel very wanted or appreciated a good deal of the time.

13. _____ I don't frequently get compliments from people except for superficial things.

14. _____ I am embarrassed when people praise me or flatter me.

15. _____ I know that there are some people who still don't like me.

16. _____ I have some personality characteristics I wish I didn't have.

17. _____ I can be overdependent on what people think of me.

18. _____ Somehow I don't feel very worthwhile or valuable.

19. _____ I am not as cheerful and easy to laugh as I wish I were.

20. _____ There are things I still feel guilty or ashamed about.

21. _____ I tend to worry about the same things over and over.

22. _____ I can be pretty sensitive and touchy about things.

23. _____ I know certain things in my past are still troublesome.

24. _____ People can really hurt me.

25. _____ I am self-conscious in conversations.

26. _____ I am uncomfortable when someone tells me they love me or need me.

1 = 1-26,	2 = 27-50,	3 = 51-77,	4 = 78-103,	5 = 104-130
High SE	Good SE	Moderate SE	Low SE	Very low SE

5. **Dependency, independence responses.** Many over-comers, especially women, have experienced a lack of dependency need fulfillment as children. Because parents didn't encourage dependency or created too much dependency, overcomers are frequently insecure and create overdependent and co-dependent relationships. Emotional dependency (ED) or attachment is a major problem with people who struggle with homosexuality. Even though you may not be sexually involved with another person, you may still hold on to someone in an emotionally dependent way.

Laura has never been able to advance in her career because she has become overly dependent and attached to Judy, an older woman in her unit at work. She says Judy is like a mother to her. Laura is continually struggling with her feelings toward Judy. She wants a great deal of her attention and feels jealous of her relationships with others. Even though others advance in their careers and earn more money, Laura remains trapped in her unit because she can't give up this relationship. Recently, Judy began talking of finding a new job herself. This made Laura depressed and very upset.

In Lori Rentzel's outstanding writing on the subject of emotional dependency, she points to these as signs of unmistakable emotional dependency:

— Frequent jealousy, possessiveness, and desire for exclusive attention.
— Prefers to spend time alone with the person.
— Becomes overly angry or irritated when the other pulls away or withdraws.
— Experiences romantic and sexual feelings for the other.
— Becomes obsessed with the other.
— Cannot see the other's faults realistically.
— Overly intimate, affectionate, and defensive with the other.[1]

Mark has an emotional attachment to Joe at work. He thinks about him continually and is preoccupied with every opportunity to see and talk with Joe. He sends Joe cards in the mail and buys him gifts. He doesn't want anyone to know of his feelings for Joe, and when Joe told another employee about the gifts, Mark was upset and angry because he felt that the gifts were a secret between them.

6. **Intimacy, closeness, affection responses.** Just touching a woman is cause for fear and anxiety for Stefano. The dates he has had with women have made him apprehensive. Getting physically close to a woman makes him feel anxious. Stefano's mother was a very overbearing woman who kept Stefano very close to her because he was an only child, and she and Stefano's father were always in conflict.

Stefano often became her support and the object of all her emotional attention. As he grew up, Stefano felt smothered by his mother. As a replacement for his father, he experienced a kind of emotional incest and would sleep in his mother's bed up until the age of eleven.

In this kind of exploitive dysfunctional family, children are often possessions, and Stefano's own needs were neglected. Now he finds it very difficult to feel sexual feelings for a woman since he had to repress his own sexual feelings for his mother for so long.

Closeness and intimacy with the opposite sex becomes very troublesome for overcomers. Such closeness with the opposite sex parent often was conflictual, painful, or a source of hurt and rejection. By allowing yourself to become open and vulnerable, the giving and receiving of affection and love can be highly threatening and anxiety producing.

Tricia, an overcomer, recently met Ted at church. He is physically attractive to her. But Ted scares her when he shows her physical affection. She feels anxious and wants to run from the relationship. She reacts to him like someone expecting to be abused or harmed. Her rejecting and harsh father often frightened her as a child. Ever since childhood, she has expected men to let her down and mistreat her. Sexual closeness with men terrifies her.

On the other hand, she sees women as gentle, caring, and safe. Every relationship she has had with women has been comfortable and without conflict. Every relationship with a man has always been a struggle.

INTIMACY ANXIETY

What is intimacy anxiety? It is the overcomer's experience of unpleasant physical and emotional sensations (and the accompanying self-thoughts and judgments) which inhibit physical and emotional closeness with another person, usually of the opposite sex. These unpleasant and inhibiting feelings may happen whenever he is around a woman; but they are especially intense whenever he feels he must behave in certain romantic and sexual ways, or when he feels that the woman has such expectations.

God has made man a wonderful being, providing him with amazing ways to cope with his world. Not the least of these is a sort of danger alarm-arousal system which, under certain situations, warns him of impending harm. His heart beats faster, his blood pressure increases, and adrenaline pumps into the blood. He may experience mild or severe anxiety symptoms such as dizziness and light-headedness, shortness of breath or a smothering sensation, rapid heartbeat, weakness, trembling, restlessness, dry mouth, trouble swallowing, headache, ringing in the ears, blurry vision, cramps, nausea, frequent urination, sweating and cold hands and feet, difficulty in concentration, nervousness and tension, and even diarrhea.

If you experience any of these reactions and symptoms when you are in an intimacy-demanding situation with the opposite sex, it indicates that your body is ready to either "fight" or "run" because you have interpreted intimacy with the opposite sex as something dangerous or for which you are unprepared and inadequate. In short, you are experiencing intimacy anxiety. Your danger-alarm arousal system is getting in the way, even though there is no real danger. This makes you uptight, scared, nervous, tense, and anxious whenever you're in those kinds of circumstances. Your danger-alarm arousal system is operating inappropriately. You have learned to respond this way automatically and unconsciously.

In the past you probably experienced intimacy with your mother or other women as frightening experiences in which you became hurt or angry or ashamed. Now, in times of closeness and intimacy with women, your danger-alarm arousal system is activated and you become anxious and phobic. You must learn—a little at a time—that you can tolerate physical and emotional closeness without becoming anxious.

One very effective way of reducing fears, anxieties, and phobias is called systematic desensitization, or SD for short.

What is SD? SD is a technique to gradually replace your intimacy anxiety with relaxation, comfort, security, joy, and even pleasure. This is done by presenting you with a series of imagined scenes, starting with the lowest anxiety-producing scene and gradually moving to the most anxiety-producing ones. SD can also be used to reduce anxiety with an actual partner. I have found this a helpful way to begin reducing intimacy anxiety.

FOR THE COUNSELOR

Getting in touch with the way your overcomer forms transferences to others is an important step in the healing of his wounded emotional area. Instruct him in this way:

First, make a list of the many people in your life. There are family members, fellow employees, church members, acquaintances, neighbors, friends, and relatives. There are casual relationships you have with sales people in stores and service personnel. List these people on a sheet of paper.

Second, reflect on your feelings and experiences with these people. Notice what feelings you have for people and the way you interact with them. Jot down some of these feelings that come to mind. One way to do that is to picture each person in your imagination and answer the question: "(person's name) makes me feel _____"

Third, notice that one or more of the six transference reactions may be taking place. See if you can spot the kind of transferences that keep coming up with people. What does this tell you about yourself?

Fourth, notice that a number of the fifteen needles are stimulated by these people and events. Again, try to identify the ones that keep coming up over and over again.

Fifth, notice which of these transferences relates almost directly to the kinds of feelings you had with your parents as a child. This is an important connection to make.

Last, how can you begin to change these automatic reactions to people so that you are not continuing these old painful and dysfunctional patterns? Usually, this is the answer to the questions: What would be the most difficult thing to say or do in relation to this person? What would be the path of most resistance in your relationship with this person?

When your overcomer speaks to the Lord, his inner adult becomes increasingly influenced by the presence and power of the Holy Spirit within him. As he engages in dialoguing with his inner parent, he will come to sort out the voice of his critical inner parent and the way that it continues to keep his inner child feeling wounded.

The child of feelings in him will be able to become emotionally separate from his critical inner parent; the enmeshment and emotional entanglement will end. Healing of the wounded area begins to take place. The deprivation complex is less frequently stimulated, and the homosexual need begins to fade into the untroublesome background of his life.

PRAYER
Father, Your Word says, "Though my father and mother forsake me, the Lord will receive me" (Ps. 27:10). Lord, receive me this day, this hour, this moment. I can no longer blame my parents, for I know that they were hurt by their parents before them. I can no longer carry this anger toward them inside of me, for I know that Your Word says, "Whoso curseth his father or his mother, his lamp shall be put out in obscure darkness" (Prov. 20:20, KJV).

Father, begin to heal this inner voice of my parent. I ask that Your Holy Spirit who dwells in my heart, help me to forgive my parents, heal them, and heal the conflict inside of me. Help me to honor my father and my mother, as You command. I ask these things in the precious and powerful name of Jesus. Amen!

---

1. Lori Thorkelson Rentzel, *Emotional Dependency: A Threat to Close Friendships* (Baltimore: Regeneration Ministries), 3.

CHAPTER NINE

TRAIN UP A CHILD: CONVERSATIONS WITH THE INNER CHILD

Hank saw his brother Richard's car parked in front of the house when he came home for lunch. For a moment, he thought it strange that Richard should be home at noon, but quickly dismissed it. When he went into the kitchen and didn't see Richard there, he became more curious. Thinking that Richard may have gotten sick at work or had an accident, he climbed the stairs to Richard's bedroom. The door was ajar, so he pushed it open, casually calling out, "Rich?"

Richard was with another guy, nude on the bed. He couldn't believe what he saw. Two men, together! A rush of anxiety and embarrassment swept over him. He turned away quickly. They hadn't seen him come in, and in his shock he quickly tried to leave unnoticed.

Then Richard saw him. "Hank," Richard called out, as Hank was closing the door, "wait a minute!" But Hank had already closed the door and was heading for the stairs.

Richard called Hank again from the partially open bedroom door, "Hank, let me explain!" But Hank was quickly descending the stairs, eager to get away. With tears in his eyes and a touch of pain in his voice, Hank could only manage to call back, "Later, later!"

They were close brothers; the only two sons of a close, small-town family. Rich was 28; Hank was 24. Hank had always looked up to Rich; sometimes even envious of his excellence in school and his talents. Rich liked Hank a lot, though he felt he was a bit spoiled and the favorite of his father.

Hank skipped lunch altogether that day. He returned to the college library and buried himself on the computer. He just wanted to stay busy. He was confused. His mind was flooded with all kinds of ugly thoughts and feelings. "My brother: a queer, a faggot, gay, homosexual? Why? How long? Any clues? Did I ever really know my brother Rich? What about Mom and Dad? Do they know? Of course not; they would die! Both such good Christian parents; leaders at church; well respected in the community. O God, what will this do to our parents? What do I say to Rich? How do we even begin to talk about this?" Just then, the phone rang.

It was Rich. "We have to talk, Hank," he said. "Tonight. I'll meet you after work. I'll pick you up, OK?"

Hank was hesitant. That same sad feeling came rushing into his throat again. Hank said, "Why, Rich, why?"

"Please, Hank, not now. Just let me explain, OK?"

After work, they drove for almost two hours. Hank got through his anger and embarrassment. Richard did most of the talking. They both cried. Later, they were too filled with feelings and remained silent for the last ten minutes before they got home.

When they got to the driveway, Hank said he wanted to pray. Rich heard his brother's love for him as he prayed for a way out of homosexuality for Rich. They agreed not to tell anyone, especially their parents. They would talk again.

The next day Rich called our ministry. Rich loved the Lord, and as we prayed it became apparent that the Lord had worked through Rich's brother to expose his sin. Now it was time to deal with his homosexuality. No more hiding. It was time to change. Rich wanted this very much. This was the day the Lord had made for Richard. He was asked to bury this Word of the Lord in his heart: "Commit thy way unto the Lord, trust also in Him, and He shall bring it to pass" (Ps. 37:5, KJV).

THERE IS A POWER IN YOU
There is a wounded area in Richard that homosexuality cannot heal. Homosexuality may gratify, but it cannot satisfy. It

will only become healed as Richard allows the Lord into this wounded area where a sensitive inner child is hiding. It is only as the Lord comes into Richard's heart that He is "able to do immeasurably more than all we ask or imagine, according to the power that is at work within us" (Eph. 3:20).

I like the discovery that Evelyn Christenson made about this verse from Ephesians 3:20. She says,

> As I repeated this verse over and over, only two words kept standing out: **according to, according to.** I puzzled over what God was trying to teach me.
>
> The verse suddenly seemed so complicated; I decided to break it down. I lumped the words "exceedingly abundantly above all that we ask or think" into a simple "all that." God can do "all that." Then it read, "Now unto Him that is able to do . . . all that . . . according to the power that worketh in us." I had it! God is able to do "all that" **ONLY** according to the power that works in **US!** I asked myself, "Don't I have God's power in me all the time?" I must have, for . . . I have Christ in me. But do I always have the same amount of God's power working in me? The answer was no. He is able to do only in accordance with, in proportion to, the measure of that power which is working in me![1]

God is doing wonderful things in Richard's life. God is able to do all kinds of wonderful things in your overcomer; but He needs and requires him to stir that power within him by faith, trust, belief, and hope in what the Lord can do. God is most able. God is most willing, but only "according to the power that is at work within us." So, stir up your overcomer's faith! Stir up his hope! Stir up that power in him! God will begin to show him his hiding, hurting inner child of painful feelings and protective defenses.

DISCOVER YOUR INNER CHILD
Say to him: When you were a child, you needed two essential things from your parents. You needed nurturing, uncondi-

tional love; and, you needed loving discipline. However, it is very likely that you received neither of these from both of your parents consistently or enough. Instead, you were in an emotionally troublesome family environment where parenting in these vital ways may have been quite inadequate.

As you became an adult, your troubled inner child of painful feelings went into hiding deep within your unconscious, where the troubled, unsettled parent-child relationship continues. This is that wounded area or deprivation complex of painful feelings and guarded defenses.

Who is this hiding inner child? Do you know him? Have you become acquainted with him? "Your inner child is the real you, your true self, that part of you that feels deeply, needs deeply, loves deeply. Your inner child consists of your feelings, your natural talents, and your creativity—the unique dimensions of your personality."[2] For our purposes, the simplest way to think of the inner child is to see him as your feelings.

Because of the painful emotional experiences you had in childhood, you have buried this little child of primitive, sensitive, even raw, feelings. "Now, years later, your inner child may still be locked inside, robbing you of a sense of self—your true identity that is composed of your unique and vital attributes."[3]

What it all amounts to is this; you are out of touch with, and you don't want to touch, or let anybody else touch, those sensitive feelings (fifteen needles). Yet, here is the very heart of your healing. The very core of your woundedness, the very center of your homosexual burden are these feelings.

Since you did not receive that unconditional love and that loving discipline you needed as a child, it is the work of your inner adult, under the presence and the power of the Holy Spirit, to bring this emotional child out of hiding; to talk with him, to comfort him, to allow him to be himself, to cherish him and love him. In other words, you need to be re-parented.

It is also important to lovingly discipline him; to help him to be tough, to see things through, to act responsibly, and to be constructive, or what I call being proactive.

LISTEN TO YOUR INNER CHILD

Your inner child is unfamiliar to you. You must get to know him. You must come to know which of those fifteen (or other) wounded emotions are hurting. Learn who you are! What do you (your inner child) cry about? What makes you sad? What makes you angry? What do you feel discouraged, overwhelmed, and defeated by?

Not having been listened to sensitively as a child, you lack a certain awareness, comfort, and control over your emotional life. Now you must start to listen and get to know yourself all over again.

How do you begin to listen to the feelings of your inner child? How do you begin to be in touch with the very feelings that are so painful?

There are four steps you can take to become aware of your feelings and to manage and live more in touch with them. However, before you can use these four steps, you will need to adopt an attitude of openness. That is, you will have to say to yourself, "I want to get to know my inner child's feelings. I truly desire to be open to whatever I'm feeling. I will not dampen or deny my feelings. I will go looking for my feelings."

Perhaps the most important attitude is this, "Whatever I'm feeling is OK. I will not judge my feelings. Feelings are OK; feelings are neutral; I will accept whatever I'm feeling for the purpose of learning more about myself."

If you are willing to adopt these important preliminary attitudes about your emotional life, you will make effective use of these four steps.

FOUR STEPS TO EMOTIONAL RENEWAL

Step One: NAME IT

Begin by looking for clues that you are feeling something. Usually, your body changes tell you that you are having a feeling. You feel stiff, your stomach gets upset, your heart beats faster, your breath becomes shorter, your shoulders tense up, you feel restless, your throat tightens, you clench your fists, you feel fatigued or stressed.

Your mood changes. You feel melancholy, unhappy, out of

sorts, withdrawn, confused, depressed, overwhelmed, very sensitive, continually irritated, or anxious. You may simply feel a vague sense of discomfort and emotional turmoil. You feel that you are under a cloud of unmotivated malaise and pressure.

Your behavior changes. You act differently. You are unkind, attacking, short and sharp with others. You withdraw, avoid, or decline to interact with others. You want to be left alone.

Once you have picked up on the clues that feelings are going on, the first thing you have to do is identify or name the feelings you are experiencing. As soon as you become aware that you are feeling something, look for a word or phrase or behavioral experience to describe it. Let's use Richard, who we met before, as an example.

Richard often feels tense and agitated at the end of a workday. After he gets home, he tries to take some time to tune into what happened during the day and what he is feeling. Richard has come to learn that when he loses touch with his feelings, especially the painful ones, it isn't long before he feels like cruising. He starts to feel that complexity of painful emotions which leaves him feeling deprived and empty, unwanted and unimportant, and he wants to be with a man.

Richard is a waiter at a busy restaurant. As he begins to reflect on his day, he realizes that he had one particular customer who upset him. The customer became loud and verbally abusive because he was displeased with his meal. Richard knows that this incident was staying with him because his body was tense, his mood was irritable, and he felt like he didn't want to talk with his roommate.

As he got in touch with these feelings, he began to name them. He knew his sensitive inner child felt humiliated, hurt, angry, embarrassed, inadequate, and demeaned. When these feelings are stimulated in Richard, he would rather push them aside and deny them, but he knows that when he does this he only gets more tense, upset, and eventually empty enough to begin looking for sexual release.

Here is how Richard began to converse with his inner child.

(IA) OK, Richard, what are you feeling?

(IC) Well, that customer really got me (I could use some very un-Christian language) "angry."

(IA) And . . . ?

(IC) That's what it was: anger, fury, annoyance.

(IA) Richard, you and I both know that "anger" never stands alone. Come on, Rich, what else were you feeling before you got angry?

(IC) Well, let's see. Before I was angry, I was getting to feel . . . ah . . . ah . . . humiliated, insulted, I guess.

(IA) Yeah, that's right! What else was going on?

(IC) That's all it was at the time, I think.

(IA) But later, what were you feeling?

(IC) On my way home from work, I was still feeling humiliated and angry and insulted. Then I think I started feeling embarrassment, some inadequacy . . .

(IA) Wait, let's just talk about that feeling of inadequacy for a minute. What were you saying to yourself that turned the anger and humiliation into a feeling of inadequacy?

(IC) Well, I guess I started to say, "You should have been more clear with the cook. You should have told the cook to leave the onions on the side. That's what the customer wanted."

(IA) Richard, that sounds like your inner parent. I hear the "should" word. You know, whenever you hear "should" or "ought to," it is most often your critical inner parent talking.

(IC) Yeah, you're right! I hear it also.

(IA) So, let's see; you felt hurt, angry, humiliated, embarrassed. You started to call yourself inadequate.

(IC) Right! Then I noticed that for the rest of the day I started to look at guys a little longer and a little stronger. I realize that looking at guys was a way of taking in something pleasurable and pleasing. It sort of made up for the hurt and inadequacy I was feeling. WOW! I see how my feelings really are tied in with homosexual attractions.

(IA) You're doing good inner dialoguing with your inner child, Richard, keep it up!

The dialogue between Richard's inner child and inner adult is an internal version of a real dialogue which I had with Richard in our counseling together. Often, I will engage my clients in the very conversations which they must learn to have within themselves. In these conversations, I am acting as the client's inner adult, while the client is acting out the voices of his inner parent and inner child. When this is done repeatedly, the client learns to internalize and reproduce these same kinds of inner dialogues.

THE DEPRIVATION COMPLEX

Your wounded area is a complexity of feelings (fifteen needles) which may begin with one dominant feeling, but always connects and stimulates other feelings. When several of these wounded feelings are activated together, the deprivation complex is experienced, and you begin to hurt so much that you look for a sexual experience to take away your pain and emptiness.

These feelings often show up in quartets, trios, or at least in pairs. In the counseling situation, Teyber says, "If the therapist acknowledges the client's current affect and invites him to explore it further, a sequence of interrelated feelings, a constellation of emotional reactions that are central to the client's conflict, will often occur together as a predictable patterned sequence."[4]

One of these patterns is the "buddies" I frequently see hanging around together in pairs, triads, or quartets. This grouping of feelings is particularly common among Christians who struggle with homosexuality. It is the sequence which was seen in Richard's experience at work: hurt, anger, guilt, depression.

He initially experiences some form of hurt (humiliation, attack, demeaned, rejected, ignored, etc.) which is not easily dismissed because of his LSE, low self-esteem. Then this hurt arouses his anger (irritation, annoyance, criticism, sarcasm, etc.). But frequently anger was suppressed or repressed in childhood; it was not allowed to be displayed. Therefore, it quickly became guilt because the anger was turned in on his sensitive inner child. When hurt-anger-guilt is held within for very long, it becomes depression or sadness.

Sometimes it is anger that is seen first with pain hiding behind it. Behind the pain is shame, insecurity, or helplessness. If you will pursue the trail of feelings, one after another, you will discover that there are several "buddies" hanging around together. In order to capture that grouping of feelings, you will need to move to a second step.

Step Two: FACE IT, FEEL IT

The next step in your dialogue with your inner child is to stay with the feelings you have named. Look at them directly. Allow them to be experienced. Get used to and "comfortable" with even the most troublesome feelings. Don't back away from them. Get to know what these feelings really feel like in your body. Let them be themselves. Don't judge them, run from them, change them, or try to even analyze them. The important thing here is to experience them; hold them, caress them, embrace them as your very own feelings. Learn to tolerate them in their pure form.

How do you do this? Beyond giving feelings a one-word name, Richard was taught in counseling to experience his feelings in several other ways. He gives his feeling a phrase description. After naming the feeling of embarrassment, he also describes it in the phrases, "I feel like two cents, I feel like a 'good-for-nothing.' " These phrases help him experience his feeling of embarrassment more deeply.

Richard was also taught to find a behavioral experience description to further feel and face his feelings. He let his inner child say, "I feel like I've been 'raped,' unmasked. I feel like crawling under a rock. I feel like someone has stepped all over my face."

Try a few of your own needles. Give phrase descriptions and behavioral experience descriptions to the following feelings:

Anxious	Ignored	Shame	Afraid
Angry	Failure	Helpless	Inadequate
Self-pity	Weak	Rejection	Victimized
Violated	Ridicule	Unloved	

Another thing Richard does to face and feel his feelings is to make sounds that seem to capture the essence of his feeling. With the feeling of embarrassment, he gets alone at home or in the privacy of his car, and exaggerates how he is feeling with sounds like, "Ooooooh . . . Ooooooh . . . Nooooo."

As he makes these sounds, he acts out his feeling in some way.

With the feeling of embarrassment, he will cover his face, bend over his shoulders and head, and shake his head from side to side.

These different ways of trying to experience and stay with his feelings enable Richard to move through the chain of feelings going on in him and to experience his feelings in greater depth.

As he stayed with his feeling of humiliation, he started to feel his embarrassment at the restaurant more. This brought a sense of shame upon him. The feeling of rejection and abuse he felt from the customer opened up feelings of loneliness and abandonment. It made him feel unimportant and worthless. He began to realize that these are all feelings from times in his childhood. Childhood memories of rejection and aloneness began to come to consciousness. This led to a deep sadness and Richard began to cry.

Self-pity seemed to follow from his sadness; then irritation, anger, and even rage. All of this led to the need to want someone to love him and comfort him and care for him. He needed to be with someone to affirm him. He felt he had to find someone soon so that he would not be alone with this deprived and empty mood any longer.

All of these things were going on in Richard the three days prior to the day he left work early, went to a cruising area, picked up a guy he knew, brought him home, and Hank walked in on them.

Now, Richard has learned to take two other steps to complete his dialogue with his inner child.

Step Three: TALK IT, TALK TO IT, TALK ABOUT IT
Now that Richard is in touch with a whole complexity of feelings, he needs to talk it through, as he felt it through in step two. He needs to expand and continue the dialogue between his inner child and inner adult.

(IA) So, Rich (his nickname as a child), talk to me about your feelings.
(IC) I really feel hurt by someone who criticizes me, like that

customer did. It must attack my self-esteem. I'm very sensitive to it.

(IA) Go on, tell me more about it!

(IC) Well, I just close off and shut down when I am made to look foolish or inadequate. And then, when it becomes anger, I can see how I have a really hard time with that feeling. I get sad almost immediately because anger turns to self-blame and guilt, and guilt is hard for me to feel.

(IA) Yeah, go on, I'm listening.

(IC) Well, guilt makes me feel like I'm bad and evil, or something.

(IA) That guilt comes from turning that anger in on your child. How about just being angry.

(IC) That's what I have a hard time with. I don't like to get angry, and I don't like to feel angry.

(IA) How come? What does anger do to you?

(IC) It makes me insecure, unsettled, anxious, nervous.

(IA) Did you get that way when your father got angry around the house, or toward you?

(IC) Oh, yes, many times! I can remember just hiding behind my mother. I must have been very fearful of him. I must have begun to feel very frightened of men from my father. That made me afraid to be a man and act like a man. WOW! That's still going on in me.

(IA) Keep talking, Rich, it's good for you!

(IC) Yeah!

The conversation continued. As Richard talks through his feelings, he notices how acceptable and comfortable he becomes with them. Even better, he notices how acceptable he becomes to himself. He starts to like himself better. He feels more secure, more in control of his emotional life. He feels stronger, more confident, and more manly.

Step Four: ACT IT, ACT ON IT

Feelings really become worked through if you complete the process of steps one, two, and three by taking some action whenever this is possible and appropriate.

One way to do that is to talk with someone about the whole experience you have had. You could talk to your "special friend," a family member or, of course, a counselor. Another good way to "actionize" your conversation between your inner child and inner adult is to write about it in a diary or journal.

Other times, the situation may call for you to actually talk to someone involved in the circumstances which provoked your inner child.

Richard may have had to talk with a fellow waiter at work, the cook, or his supervisor. He also now talks to Hank more often.

Since the trail of feelings led Richard to some painful childhood memories, he could choose to speak with his parents about some of those experiences. This could open up troublesome relational areas, but it could also begin to heal them. Remember Romans 8:28!

A GUARDED PORCUPINE

As you begin to use these four steps to get in touch with your sensitive inner child, you will experience a strong resistance within you. You have become accustomed to being a person who protects these sensitive and painful feelings, and you may find it very uncomfortable to touch them. You have been accustomed to protecting this vulnerable area by acting like a guarded porcupine. Haven't you seen what a porcupine does when it is under attack? A porcupine shoots out pointed needles to keep others away when he feels threatened. You resemble a porcupine defending himself against attack (see diagram #1).

As I counsel wounded Christians who struggle with homosexuality, I find they frequently protect their wounded areas by using one or more of three protective reactions. All three are somewhat dysfunctional and defensive. They are fight reactions, flight reactions, and fright reactions.

THREE PROTECTIVE REACTIONS

1. **Fight reactions.** Some people have a protective stance in life of always fighting others. They are suspicious, defensive, attacking, abrasive, antagonistic, angry, irritated, distrusting, hostile, sarcastic, cynical, ridiculing, criticizing, gossiping, backbiting, name-calling, blaming, and demeaning.

DIAGRAM 1   Close-Up of Wounded Area and Porcupine Guards or Protective Reactions

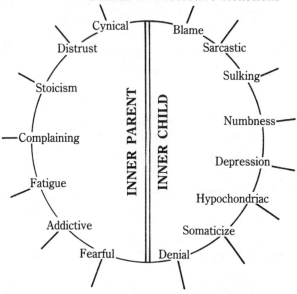

They often feel that people are the cause of their problems. They blame others, find fault with others, criticize others, and are often distrusting of others' motives. As much as they need to have personal and intimate emotional contact with others, they keep people at arms' length. The threat of being hurt and disappointed again is so frightening that it is safer, so they feel, to forego all intimacy and closeness.

2. **Flight reactions.** You may be a person who protects his wounded feelings by avoiding and escaping. Your unconscious stance is, "I won't let it bother me." You take a position of denial of what you are feeling: procrastination, inaction, stoicism, running from conflict, placating others, not asserting yourself as you need to, making excuses, being devious and manipulative at times.

You may remain insensitive to others, and engage in emotional withdrawal, depersonalization, and indifference to deep emotional responses. Often you may end up sulking, holding out, not giving in, whining, complaining, and self-pity. This is often the passive-aggressive person who can also be a workaholic, perfectionist, compulsive, and addictive.

3. **Fright reactions.** This third defensive, protective reac-

tion has an unconscious stance of, "I'm unable to handle it." It is a protective position which turns over many of its emotional pressures to the body. The unsolved emotional needling of the wounded area is "somaticized." This means that emotions are converted into physical, bodily symptoms.

You may experience headaches, backaches, stomach troubles, depression, chronic fatigue, or continuous burnout. When this protective reaction is severe, a person may suffer from ulcers, colitis, and other stress-related illnesses.

It is not uncommon to see this person using addictive substances which numb the body to relieve stress and pressure. This person may also have phobic fears and anxieties, and can be somewhat of a hypochondriac and psychosomatic.

PROACTING: DOING WHAT'S RIGHT

You probably recognize some of these protective reactions in yourself. Remember, they are all ways of protecting or defending your sensitive, wounded emotions. Because they do protect you in that way, you will find it difficult to change them or give them up. Yet, each one interferes with mature and constructive emotional expression and with interpersonal relationships. Furthermore, they all keep you isolated behind a wall of remoteness from others, depriving you of the normal intimacy you need with both males and females. This is the most tragic aspect of these protective reactions.

In order to have a deeper satisfying emotional life, with freedom from homosexual compromise, you need to dismantle and reduce these protection reactions. Instead of protecting yourself through Fight, Flight, or Fright, you need to do what is Right for your inner child. Doing what is right is proacting.

Proacting means to make positive, constructive, and forceful responses to overcoming these three protective reactions and coming to grips with your wounded emotions. It means to make the choice of "most" resistance instead of "least" resistance whenever possible. It means doing what does not come naturally. It means going against the grain of your protective reactions and your sensitive emotions. It means forcing yourself to overcome the tendency to continue protecting yourself and hiding your sensitive emotions. It means engaging in actions and behaviors which counteract what you have always done before. Here is how Richard has started to be proactive in his life.

Richard went to a singles group at his church where he met Susan. They began to spend time together and date. One night, as they were driving home from a party, Richard came to an abrupt stop behind the car in front of him. Susan became frightened and angrily snapped at Richard, "What's the matter with you, Rich? Why don't you drive more carefully?" Her voice and body showed annoyance and criticism. At the time, Richard simply said, "The guy in front of me stopped short. I'm sorry! What did you expect me to do?" Susan became silent and turned to look out the window for the rest of the trip home. She got out of the car quickly and they said "good night" to each other without further comment. As Richard drove home, he was filled with conflicting, troubled feelings.

That night he went to bed agitated and disturbed. The next morning, he began this inner conversation with himself.

(IC) I feel terrible! I am angry, annoyed, discouraged, and humiliated. I feel rejected. I feel like a failure. O God, I can't handle this.

(IP) You know you are not able to have a good relationship with a woman. You are still so immature and childish. Why don't you grow up! There you go, failing again. You're so inadequate. You just don't have what it takes to be a man with a woman.

(IC) You're right. Why did I ever think I could date or have a serious relationship with a woman? I'm so babyish.

(IA) Richard, Richard, I'm calling you! Richard, you have been ignoring me. How about giving me some equal time in this conversation?

(IP) No! Get out! You're just a happy idealist. There is nothing you can say to make things better. Can't you see he's hurting. Why don't you just leave him alone. You only create false hopes for him.

(IA) Be still! Richard, let me remind you of something, "I feel sure that the One who has begun His good work in you will go on developing it until the day of Jesus Christ" (Phil. 1:6,

PH). And let me remind you, "Him who by His power within us is able to do infinitely more than we ever dare to ask or imagine" (Eph. 3:20, PH). And, Romans 8:28!

(IC) I hear You, Lord, I hear You! Thank You, Lord Jesus!

(IA) Now, let's get going. In this situation with Susan, what have I taught you to do in such situations?

(IC) I know, I have to start proacting. OK! I know I can do something constructive here. I will not let this defeat me. "I can do all things through Christ who strengthens me. Greater is He that is in me, than he that is in the world." What is the mature thing to do? What is the most honest and truthful thing to do here? What is the hardest thing to do here? I know what it is. It's to go to Susan and really talk out what happened last night. But, I'm afraid!

(IA) Talk about your fear, get in touch with your fear. What does it feel like?

(IC) Well, it feels like . . . like . . . scary, anxiety.

(IA) What does it feel like in your body?

(IC) It feels like a thing in my chest. A jumpy kind of breathing.

(IA) OK! Let's get that feeling to pass. How about breathing deeply; go ahead, do it!

(IC) Yes, that's better. I'm relaxing now.

(IA) What do you expect to happen when you talk to Susan?

(IC) I'll start getting fearful again; I might even cry.

(IA) And, what's so bad about that?

(IP) You'll look like a fool, like a weak man!

(IC) Yeah, that's right! Then she'll know I'm a baby.

(IA) Do men cry? Can men show their true feelings, Richard? Richard, haven't you learned that it is better to reveal than to conceal?

(IC) Yes, I have. I'm going to do it. I'm going to talk to Susan.

Richard has broken through his flight protective reaction and allowed his real feelings of fear and criticism to be exposed. When he does this with Susan, all may or may not go wonderfully well, yet, he is engaging her in an open and honest relationship. He is proacting, and this will change his wounded area and defensive guardedness. He is doing just those things which preserve his integrity, heal his wounded emotions, raise his self-esteem, accept himself, honor God, and value Susan.

Whenever your overcomer acts forcefully, maturely, ethically, morally, assertively, and reasonably, he will change. He will heal. He will begin to feel whole and manly. He will start to see the end of the homosexual attraction and desire. The big "H" will start to fade into the background of his life.

FOR THE COUNSELOR

You can see the importance for your overcomer to be in touch with the inner child of feelings and give up his usual protective reactions. I think you can see the importance of proacting.

When he begins to allow the Holy Spirit to operate through his inner adult to converse with his inner parent, and to nurture and discipline his inner child, a new self-image and self-esteem begins to emerge. Homosexual attractions and temptations will begin to lose their drawing power. He will find himself able to turn from homosexual preoccupations more easily. He will develop an inner strength and control which overcomes the deprivation complex.

Much of the work in counseling overcomers has to do with providing them with a model of a mature, reasonable, and rational adult voice in their lives. Because his own inner adult voice is often overwhelmed by his more dominant critical inner parent and inner child voices, the overcomer needs to internalize his counselor's Spirit-led adult voice until he makes it his own.

One most important way for him to hear that inner adult voice is when you, the counselor, invite him to use the four steps of emotional renewal over and over again. Consistently doing this begins to heal the sensitive inner child and wounded area of painful feelings and protective reactions.

He begins to let down his wall of guards and allows his sensitive emotions to come out of hiding where they can be seen and touched, accepted and healed. As you create a relationship of trust and acceptance, he will increasingly risk exposing his real self to himself and to you. He begins to like himself; feel significant, worthwhile, and secure. He begins to see himself as truly free in Christ Jesus.

"Freedom is what we have, Christ has set us free! Stand, then, as free men, and do not allow yourselves to become slaves again. . . . As for us, our hope is that God will put us right with Him, and this is what we wait for, by the power of God's Spirit working through our faith. . . . And those who belong to Christ Jesus have put to death their human nature, with all its passions and desires. The Spirit has given us life; He must also control our lives" (Gal. 5:1, 5, 24-25, GNB).

1. Evelyn Christenson, *What Happens When God Answers* (Waco: Word, 1986), 37.
2. Richard W. Dickinson, *The Child in Each of Us* (Wheaton, Ill.: Victor Books, 1989), 13.
3. J. Patrick Gannon, *Soul Survivors: A New Beginning for Adults Abused as Children* (New York: Prentice Hall, 1989), 64.
4. Edward Teyber, *Interpersonal Process in Psychotherapy* (Chicago: The Dorsey Press, 1988), 85.

CHAPTER TEN

IN DUE SEASON WE SHALL REAP: A BIBLE STUDY SUMMARY

There is an end. There is wholeness. There is freedom. The Lord purposes to complete the work which He began in your overcomer. Therefore, "Let us not become weary in doing good, for at the proper time we shall reap a harvest if we do not give up" (Gal. 6:9).

In this chapter, I want to summarize the learning in this book and help your overcomer form a practical plan of action; a plan of daily self-therapy that heals.

First, please turn to Matthew 21:23-32. I'd like you to read it through once.

CHANGE TAKES EFFORT

One day Jesus was teaching in the temple. The chief priests and elders challenged Him by asking, "By what authority are You doing these things?" He responded by asking them about the origin of the authority by which John baptized. Whatever answer they gave, He knew they would convict themselves and would have to face the fact that Jesus was the Messiah, and that this was the basis of His authority. But they, seeing the decision which He was forcing them to make, backed out altogether and said, "We don't know!"

The truth is that they should have said, "We will not decide!" It was not a matter of not understanding, but of being unwilling to change. They were unwilling to make a decision for Jesus. They were unwilling to accept His authority as

God, and make the decision which that acceptance implied.

We come back to the first question of the first chapter: "Do I have to change?" You know you have to change and you want to change. This book should have given you ample evidence that change is possible. All that remains is the question: "Will you do the things you must in order to change?"

Change is hard. No one likes to change. We all like to maintain the status quo. We all resist change. It is easier to remain with what is painfully familiar, than to engage in unknown change. The momentum is to keep letting the weed seeds sprout and grow. It takes effort to plant the corn seeds of healing, water them, till the soil, pull out weeds, and cultivate the plants. In due season, however, your overcomer will reap the harvest, if he engages in the daily self-therapy that heals. Share this Bible lesson with your overcomer.

TWO SONS

Because the Pharisees were unwilling to take a stand and make a decision, Jesus told them the Parable of the Two Sons. Jesus often told parables when He wanted a message to sink in and convict His listeners. See if that is what happens to you!

Both these sons were imperfect sons to their father because both were not completely in accord with their father's will. Human fathers can be inconsistent and let you down. Maybe yours did just that to you.

The first son set his will against his father's, but finally carried out his will by his actions. The second professed to be in compliance with his father's will, to the father's face at least, but by his actions he showed that he would not obey. Which of the two are you?

Jesus clearly preferred the son who, even though once ambivalent and resistant, finally went into the vineyard to work. How about you? Will you go into the vineyard and really work, even though you may be discouraged and unsure of the results? Are you going to act on what you have learned in these chapters? Or, like the second son, are you going to say yes with your lips, but refuse to do the hard work needed to change homosexuality? Jesus says, "Son, go and work today in My vineyard."

This is not a question! It is a directive; a command. Jesus says you must begin to work to change homosexuality. It's time to take action. He is telling you to do it. Start taking action today! Begin engaging in the daily self-therapy that heals.

Notice: He calls you "Son." You have a changed heart. You are saved. You are reborn. You are one of His own. You are a family member. He is your Father and you are His son. You always needed a father. He always wanted you as a son. Since you are His son, you are entitled to all your Father's inheritance, all of His finest gifts (Luke 11:13; Gal. 4:7). Do you realize what it means to be a real son? This Father wants to really care for you and love you. Do you realize who it is that is your Father? Do you know the Lord God Almighty as your Father? Get to know Him as your Father! I invite you; I implore you; get to know God as your Father. Make a word study of "Father" and the fatherhood of God in the Bible. You will come to understand what it means to be His son. "Every good gift and every perfect gift is from above, and cometh down from the Father of lights" (James 1:17, KJV).

Notice, He says "Go." He doesn't say "stay still," or "wait and see," or "think about working awhile more," or "philosophize about the change process a little." He says GO! Get going! Move! Change what you have been doing, or not doing, to what you have learned to do in this book! Change your position! Resist the momentum to stay where you are! Move!

Notice, He says, "Go and work." Work! Not only do you have to start making some movement and get going, but you have to work at it. It is going to be work. It will take some effort. Things have got to change in your life. You need to make room for some new ways of doing things.

Notice, He says, "Son, go and work today." Today! Not when you just feel like it. Not when you think it's convenient and pleasant. Today! This is the day which the Lord has made for you (Ps. 118:24). This is your day to begin. This day has your name on it. You wouldn't have come to this book and read this far if you didn't want to start working today. There is a daily work to do.

Notice, He says, "Go . . . in." Go in! Enter in! Listen to the meaning of the word *in* in these words. Understand what the word *in* means!

> Remain in Me, and I will remain in you. No branch
> can bear fruit by itself; it must remain in the vine.
> Neither can you bear fruit unless you remain in
> Me. I am the vine, you are the branches. If a man
> remains in Me, and I in him, he will bear much
> fruit; apart from Me you can do nothing. If you
> remain in Me and My words remain in you, ask
> whatever you wish, and it will be given to you
> (John 15:4-7).

"In My vineyard." Whose vineyard? The Lord's vineyard. This is His place where you are called to work. A vineyard is a place of cultivation where valuable crops are grown. That's why it is often walled off and protected with a watchtower and guard. It is a place where the Lord cultivates His choicest crops; and that's you. It's a place that needs planting, weeding, cutting, pruning, fertilizing, pulling out, feeding, and picking. It's the Lord's vineyard. He will wall you in within Himself and protect you there. He will build a tower in your heart and watch over you there. "What more could I have done for My vineyard than I have done for you?" (see Isa. 5:4) "For You have been my refuge, a strong tower against the foe" (Ps. 61:3).

Now, one more time, look at John 15:4-7. This time place your own name in the blanks. Read this out loud! Hear it being spoken to you personally!

"_____ , remain in Me, and I will remain in you. A branch cannot bear fruit by its own efforts _____ . You must remain in the vine. Neither can you _____ bear fruit, unless you _____ remain in Me. I am the vine; _____ , you are the branches. If you _____ , remain in Me, and I in you _____ , you will bear much fruit. Apart from Me _____ you can do nothing. If you _____ , remain in Me, and My words remain in you _____ , you can ask anything you wish, and it will be given to you."

THE DAILY SELF-THERAPY THAT HEALS
How will your overcomer bring all the various instruction from this book into a practical plan of daily work?

Having worked with numerous overcomers, I know that the time spent in counseling sessions is not enough to produce steady progress. Your overcomer must commit himself to daily efforts specifically designed toward homosexual healing. Those who want to accelerate their growth must commit themselves to the daily self-therapy that heals.

Maybe your overcomer has already begun to implement much of what is in this book. Whether he has or not, he should see the importance of a daily commitment to a plan that yields to the power of the Holy Spirit to change his life and conform him to the image of Jesus Christ.

Reorientation therapy involves making external and internal changes. When these are accomplished, your overcomer will see progressive and substantial change over a period of one to three years. Some of these are short-range goals and others are ongoing longer-range ones. Instruct your overcomer in this way.

SHORT-RANGE THINGS TO DO

Commit yourself to accomplish the following ten things, to the extent that it is possible, within the next month. This also serves as a checklist for those who have already begun to work on overcoming homosexuality.

1. Eliminate all pornographic materials that may be in your possession.

2. Join a good Bible-believing and preaching church.

3. Sever all homosexual relationships and emotional attachments. You must break these spiritual bondages decisively and proactively. No excuses please!

4. If you have been sexually active, have yourself medically tested for the HIV virus (AIDS) or other sexually transmitted diseases. This may cause you fear and anxiety. However, doing this will bring home to you, in a forceful manner, that your high-risk lifestyle was self-destructive. You need this reminder as an incentive.

5. Get active in a local ministry for overcomers or seek a telephone or letter support person from a nearby ministry.

6. Find reading materials on overcoming homosexuality by both secular and Christian authors. Learn as much as you can about homosexuality.

7. Find that "special friend" at church or elsewhere. Eventually tell this person about your past, and ask him to keep you accountable to him by praying with you regularly.

8. Begin the thirty-day daily log, reporting on those five areas which are listed in chapter 5.

9. Memorize the five verses (or others) in chapter 5.

10. Write out your own history of homosexual development through the six stages. In doing this, the Lord will inevitably show you things that need healing from your past. For instance, He may show you that you still have a spirit of abandonment or rejection or anger or unforgiveness. He may reveal to you, to your great surprise, that you were sexually or physically abused. He may reveal instances and memories of times when you were immobilized with fear and anxiety. He may show you that your inner child is still crying inside.

ONGOING THINGS TO DO

1. **Daily prayer.** You should set aside from ten to thirty minutes each day for quiet daily prayertime with the Lord. Be faithful to this.

2. **Church.** Your participation in weekly church provides you with fellowship of supportive relationships, feeds you with good biblical preaching and teaching, and gives you a consistent opportunity to worship God.

3. **Bible study and meditation.** Begin making a weekly Bible study, starting with the Book of James. I also recommend several other passages for Bible meditation. In order to do this consistently, you may want to attend a Bible study or home fellowship group.

4. **Overcomer's ministry.** After finding a local ministry for Christians who are overcoming homosexuality, attend regularly for at least six months to a year. Some ministries have ongoing training programs and seminars. You may also want to attend the national Exodus conference. This conference will bless you enormously.

5. **Conversations with the Lord.** These conversations will flow into your prayer and worship life. I focused on seven attributes of God that should help you view Him correctly and speak to Him in those spiritual attitudes which open the doors to God's grace and strength.

6. **Conversations with your inner parent.** I focused on six relational transferences; those unconscious and habitual ways of relating and responding to people which stimulate your inner parent voice. You should practice the exercise suggested at the end of the chapter frequently.

7. **Conversations with your inner child.** I spoke about the importance of being in touch with your inner child voice by engaging the four steps of emotional healing which help you work through your wounded emotions. I also pointed out the kinds of defensive postures or protective reactions you may use to guard that wounded area, and the need to proact. Review this material and begin these proactive conversations and behaviors regularly.

8. **Meet with your special friend.** It is most important to meet with this supportive and trusted friend at least every other week. I would suggest that this person be a same-sex, non-gay or ex-gay older person, or a married couple. This person will keep you motivated, encouraged, and accountable. Even if you are working with a counselor, I believe there is a need for this kind of relationship. You need someone with whom you can have vital contact regularly.

9. **Other relationships.** You should provide time for weekly fellowship with good Christian peers (male and female). These should be primarily social, recreational, fun, and relaxing times. You need these relationships and experiences in order to learn or relearn social skills with both sexes, and to avoid burnout.

10. **Counseling.** Find a good Christian counselor. It is through professional Christian counseling that many internal changes will take place. If you work with your counselor for one to three years, you will have someone who will help you improve your interior self-talk and renew your self-esteem and gender identity security as well as help you develop a plan for overcoming intimacy anxiety with opposite-sex relationships.

If you will commit yourself to this plan of daily, weekly, monthly self-therapy, you will experience substantial healing. You will begin to see that "All things work together for good for those who love God and are called according to His purpose" (Rom. 8:28).

All things will begin to work together for your good. This is the promise which God makes to you because you love Him; because you have been called to this journey of healing, according to His purpose. This is what God promised.

God Promised
God did not tell me
Only roses would grow.
That I'd find no sorrow,
On the path I must go.

But He promised to be there,
Each step of the way,
Providing a way to escape,
The temptations each day.

His grace all sufficient,
Daily to see me through.
He'd help me to conquer,
And be victorious too.[1]

FOR THE COUNSELOR
Many people who are very committed to overcoming homosexuality, fail to do the daily and weekly work which is needed to produce sustained progress. Healing homosexuality is more like making steady turtle tracks, not lion leaps. Each day is a day which the Lord has made for them. Each day has numerous opportunities for change and healing and growth when your overcomer knows what to look for and how to seize the opportunities for change and healing.

Help your overcomer really get organized in his change efforts. Don't settle for good intentions and high ideals only. The recovery process can be overwhelming at times. He can easily get offtrack and lose sight of where he is going. He is emotionally and spiritually vulnerable to discouragement. Setbacks will inevitably occur. They should be seen as lessons for learning and improvement. Some of the most valuable changes come about after a setback. Goals will change as he goes along. He will see new areas to tackle. The Lord will be with you, the counselor, and your overcomer showing you both each new step to take. Keep in prayer! Stay close to the inner voice of the Holy Spirit! Say to your overcomer: "Son, go and work today in my vineyard. In due season you will reap the harvest. In due time, you will be victorious too."

Let David tell you about the journey of healing which he was called to, and how he is inheriting what was promised to him by the Lord.

Father, I thank You that You have brought me through this time of learning and discovery. Father, You know how much I desire to be healed of homosexuality. You know that in the deepest part of my heart, I want to please You. Father, I'm glad that You said, "Man looketh on the outward appearance, but the Lord looketh on the heart" (1 Sam. 16:7, KJV).

Jesus, my journey is only beginning, and I need Your help each day. Renew me in my inner man through Your Holy Spirit. In Your precious and powerful name, I pray. Amen.

---

1. © Dottlee Duggan Reid, "God Promised" in *Best Loved Poems* (New Rochelle: Salesian Missions, 1983), 106.

CHAPTER ELEVEN

HOMOSEXUAL NO MORE: DAVID'S TESTIMONY

David would be the first to admit that he is still learning how to be a farmer. At the time of this publication David continues to work hard at becoming a new person. He is removing layer after layer of those protective reactions and plowing through the soil of his wounded emotional life. Sometimes it seems to him that all he is doing is the preparation work of tilling the soil, removing the rocks and boulders, and digging out the weeds—the hard work of relinquishing the old man. Remaking the inner man and doing the deeper work of healing is painful. But David has longer periods of emotional stability, greater freedom from addictive behaviors of all kinds, and an increasing absence of the homosexual preoccupation.

David's testimony deserves to be heard, not because he is the most healed or the most successful overcomer I have worked with, but because he is one of the most committed and persevering persons I know. In his own words listen to how he is inheriting what the Lord has promised.

I MUST ACCEPT RESPONSIBILITY
Recovery is possible, and recovery is real. This is a story of hope for those who struggle with this problem. You can recover your heterosexuality, which has been lost or broken.

As you read this story, you may be tempted to interpret it as an indictment against my family and against others who may have hurt me and contributed to this problem.

I reveal this story, not to blame or punish my family, but to celebrate the healing which has not only occurred within me, but also in them, and among us. This is the story of how understanding and forgiveness of others, especially family members, can lead to a richer appreciation of them, as fallen and less-than-perfect human beings. It can lead to a fuller honoring of my parents, which we are commanded to do.

Further, an exposé such as this ultimately reveals some things that I would prefer to remain private. A friend to whom I confided my story, pointed out that while my family may have been responsible for the inner disturbance which led me to behave this way, I was responsible for the consequences of my actions as an adult.

How correct she is! This is a story where the primary blame and responsibility rests with me. I risked contracting a fatal disease; I risked arrest and scandal each time I engaged in sexual activity in public places; I risked loss of my livelihood, indeed, loss of my home, as I continued to pander to the needs of a drug-addicted partner.

It is my hope that not only those who are struggling with this problem will begin their victories, but that, through my story, parents and others will learn ways to spare their children this burden.

IN THE BEGINNING

I was born in New Jersey in 1951. My parents moved to the community in the postwar flight to the suburbs.

My father lived in town since he was two years old. My grandfather, the product of an old New England family, had been transferred by his company from Boston to New York. His wife, my grandmother, was also from an established old family in New England.

My father was an only child, born after ten years of marriage. He used to boast that he was "Daddy's draft exemption" during the first World War. The U.S. did enter the war in April 1917, but married men with children were not drafted.

But I believe that there was a germ of truth to my father's joking. I knew my grandfather, and he was a hard, stern, unyielding man. Dad wanted desperately to study journalism and communications when he graduated from high school in 1935. The Depression had not touched his family, and money was not a concern, but Grandfather insisted that Dad attend a prestigious university and study business as he had. His rationale was that radio, which my dad wanted to study, was only a "passing fancy" and a frivolous pursuit. How ironic that by 1950, radio doubled in its scope and reach with the invention of television.

Dad dropped out of college, went to war, married the girl next door, and earned his living as a teamster. He has a brilliant, sharp mind, and while he never speaks of his feelings, I believe that there was always a regret that he was dissuaded from pursuing his dream of radio.

Six months after my mom moved to the same suburban street in 1933, her father died of a stroke. He was forty-three. His passing was to become a dominant theme in Mother's life; to this day, she has never dealt with the abandonment she felt over his death.

Mom was left with the responsibility of caring for the home and her rebellious younger brother, while my grandmother found secretarial work in New York. Without paternal influence, her younger brother had to be sent to a private preparatory school where he could be closely supervised. He and my mother have not communicated since 1965.

In 1946, Dad married Mom and moved in with her, her mother, and brother Bill. My uncle married and left in 1950. My grandmother lived in a nursing home from 1978 until her death in 1985.

THE CONSEQUENCES OF SURGERY

Approximately six months after my birth, the right side of my head began to swell. Further examination revealed hydrocephalus, the accumulation of fluid within the skull. Surgery was performed to relieve the pressure. I was fortunate, in that, unlike some who need repeated surgical procedures to correct the condition, one surgery was all that was required. However, there were two consequences to the surgery that had a long-term impact: one which was quickly apparent, and one which would not surface for twenty years.

The immediate consequence of the surgery was total paralysis on the left side. This necessitated leg braces and daily physical therapy until I was twelve years old. Today, I have a modest limp on my left foot, but no other discernible handicap.

Young boys, being boys, did not accept a peer whose mobility was limited by leg braces. I was very self-conscious about the leg braces and the other kids knew it. At a point when I was trying to reach out to others my age, I endured a daily ritual of mocking and teasing. Frequently, I was beaten; on occasion I was dragged and placed in precarious positions from which I could not extricate myself.

More often than not, I went home in tears to be comforted by my mother and to be put through the daily ritual of physical therapy. How I came to hate that brace and all it represented. Mom tried to reason with the neighborhood parents but all to no avail.

Periodically, I had to go to an orthopedic surgeon in New York for review. These ghastly trips were incomplete without requisite visits to Bloomingdale's, Saks, and Gimbel's. This, I suppose, was Mother's reward, but for me it only prolonged the agony of hearing about how important it was to do the daily physical therapy, even though there would always be a residual limp.

I don't recall an occasion when Dad was with us when we went to New York. I don't recall an occasion when Dad was even present during daily physical therapy. I do not recall any time when Dad ever intervened for me when I was having a bad day on the streets with other children.

THE PERFECT STUDENT
Failing in my attempts to find acceptance by the other boys in the neighborhood, I directed my energies to academic achievement. And what a success I was! With the exceptions of art and physical education, I was a star pupil from the first grade on. Much of my insatiable curiosity had been encouraged by my mother, who not only read traditional fairy (no pun intended) stories, but conversed with me about art, politics, and current affairs. We sat together and went through *Life* magazine page by page. She would tell me fascinating stories about President Eisenhower and Senator McCarthy, and problems in Eastern Europe.

Year after year, I charmed my way through school, earning the praise of my teachers, the admiration of my parents and grandmother, and the contempt of my peers.

I was determined to be perfect! In junior high, I was sometimes punished with everyone else, even if I was completely innocent. When these universal punishments were imposed, neither Mother nor Father intervened to defend me. In high school, I continued my quest for perfection. I was valedictorian of my class, had a long list of student activities — service organizations, student council, yearbook editor-in-chief, even a varsity letter in track for managing the county championship squad.

In the locker room, after physical education, I had my first feelings of attraction for men and the first repulsion that something was terribly wrong. The football players had tight stomachs, strong legs and chests that were expansive. The cross-country runners and basketball players were lean and trim. They all had body hair, which I lacked. I, on the other hand, was a mess! I was uncoordinated, awkward, and too heavy. My lack of hair and physique only distanced me from them further.

My body hair started to grow, but I was nevertheless repelled by it. Lacking in these physical ways led me to develop what became my adult character. I was flamboyant and outrageous. I would do anything to get a laugh. Much of my posturing was effeminate, and most of the humor made fun of my deficient athletic prowess. I was given the nickname "Crusher," and took on the role of mascot to the boys who were revered and admired.

I had one homosexual encounter in high school. One day, a very effeminate boy named Dennis talked me into undressing in his bedroom. We masturbated each other to climax. As fascinated as I was, I vowed never to do anything so repulsive again.

COLLEGE AWAKENINGS

I graduated from high school in 1969 and headed for a prestigious college in Eastern Pennsylvania. I was academically well prepared for college, but socially I was an outcast. I graduated in the top 15 percent of my class and won the prize for excellence in economics.

I desperately wanted to belong to a fraternity, but I easily fell into the familiar high school roles of clown and buffoon. I got laughs and attention but not respect and admiration. I was finally accepted into a fraternity and quickly took on the administrative tasks which gave me some security. The closeness and camaraderie with fellow fraternity brothers still eluded me.

These college years were filled with even more doubts about my sexuality. I was propositioned twice by men, but never yielded. I became angry and fascinated by beautifully formed male gods, desiring to be with them, to satisfy them sexually, even just to touch them, and yet frightened by the truth—that I did not have appropriate responses to women.

It all seemed so pointless. The Scripture was emphatic on the issue of homosexuality—and as long as I was celibate, I wasn't gay. But the feelings were so indescribable and intense. I wanted to be fulfilled. I prayed for female companionship to "cure" me, but my feelings about myself were so misshapen I couldn't relate in any minimal way to women, much less relate to them sexually. God began to drift away or, more correctly, I began to drift away from Him.

SLOWLY COMING OUT

After graduate school I moved to a Connecticut city, took a job with a small civil engineering firm for three years, and was very alone most of the time and lonely.

I began drinking and wondered what was wrong with me. About the time of my thirtieth birthday, I began to come out a little. I started frequenting adult book stores and buying hard core pornography. I started to openly look at gay material and watch gay movies in the video booths.

By 1983, I left the engineering firm and went into business for myself after passing the most strenuous professional CPA exam the second time. With my MBA and CPA I began to develop numerous clients. I was in a cycle of exhilaration and despair. Tax seasons were wonderful. I worked hard, was revered as long as clients got sizable refunds, and felt reasonably good about myself, I told myself.

The drinking and the homosexual fantasy became stronger. I gained weight and stopped exercising. I became careless about my client appointments, neglected my appearance and housekeeping, my fantasy life was now insatiable, and I actively thought about suicide. I started calling telephone lines where men talk homosexual talk to each other and masturbate while on the phone. I made my first trips to parking areas where homosexuals "cruise" other gays, but I never made contact.

I came to believe the gay activists who said that I was born gay and nothing would change that. I begged God to deliver me from the burden. My life became a whirlwind of depression, anger, rage, confusion, and desperate loneliness. Oh, the loneliness! Week after week I spent whole days and nights alone. There were times when I went for three full days without hearing another human voice.

FINALLY OUT!

New Year's Eve 1986. New Year's Eve had ceased to be special for me. It only seemed to magnify the loneliness and desperation I felt. I greeted 1987 at the home of a couple who were clients, two or three other couples, a few single women, and Bob. I had met Bob through the hosts, and he too was a client of mine. The party broke up at 1 A.M. and I went home, alone and intoxicated.

At 2:30 A.M., Bob called and asked if I had any Scotch. When I said yes, he told me to bring it over and we could watch videos. As I drove over to Bob's I was certain that cocktails and conversation were not the evening's main activity.

I had known Bob three years. I knew he had been married, but had never dated steadily. There was also an intensity in his voice that was unmistakable.

Bob greeted me at the door dressed only in a bathrobe. Within thirty minutes I had lost my virginity.

Now I finally had come out! It was then that I had to admit that I was homosexual.

INTO THE LIFE

Once the barrier of sexual contact was down, I was free to enter the life. I could no longer hide behind the veneer of being straight.

Bob would call me on occasion. Normally, he would call me in the middle of the night, drunk or on coke. My duty was to pick him up more booze or cocaine in exchange for sex. All in all, an uplifting wholesome way to spend an evening, wouldn't you say?

THEN JIMMY

I met Jimmy in April while cruising. He was young, dark, slender, all the things I came to idolize as perfect masculinity. However, Jimmy was a hustler. But I let him follow me home when he said he needed a "few bucks" because I was so alone and desperate for affection. This was the beginning of a two-year relationship.

Our relationship was at first, and thereafter, one of prostitute and john. He was paid for sex, though I wanted to believe he was my lover, companion, and friend. Later, I learned that I was only one of some ten or twelve clients Jimmy serviced regularly.

In the beginning it was pleasurable. I paid him and that was that. He told me he cared about me and listened intently when I counseled him to get off drugs and get a legitimate job and place to live.

After a few months, I became his rescuer. I scored his coke for him, he stayed over more frequently, and he began cleaning the house and running errands for me.

In the meantime, I began withdrawing from friends. After every encounter I became depressed for a few days and vowed there would be no repeats. I was short-tempered, fearful of being caught, anxious about scoring drugs, and I began drinking heavily that winter. In short, I became a slovenly mess. I began to think of suicide again.

TURNING BACK TOWARD THE FATHER'S HOUSE

I would cry out to the Lord in anger, "I don't know why You made me gay and are putting me through this hell, but make it stop. If You do, I will believe again." Then, I would begin planning the car accident that would end my life.

In the midst of this darkness, there was one ray of hope. She was a Catholic client of mine. Though she was going through a difficult financial time, Tara always had an optimistic outlook and serenity. There was a portrait of Christ on her wall and a Bible on her desk that she picked up and referred to frequently.

One day I began to think, and think hard. The Scriptures are emphatic about helping the weak, the poor, the widowed, the orphans, the sick — all conditions beyond the control of the person. Homosexuality is not in that group. In fact, homosexual behavior is clearly condemned in Scripture. I began working this through like I was working on a business problem.

"Therefore," I said, "homosexuality is optional. The Lord, being a merciful God, would not make someone gay, then condemn the very behavior with which the person was born." I kept reasoning this out. "Therefore, if I was born gay, the Scriptures would admonish Christians to be loving, charitable, and accepting of those suffering with homosexuality. Therefore, I was not born gay and there must be a solution, there must be a way out!

"Lord," I prayed, "I don't understand this, but I don't want to be gay. I don't want this lifestyle. But this is not Your doing. It must be something else. I beg You, Lord, show me the way out."

GOD LOOKETH UPON THE HEART

Ten days later, yes, ten days later, I saw the advertisement in the local paper. It said, "Gay and Christian? There is a way out of homosexuality. Hope Ministries." O God! There it was! As I changed my prayer in the way I did, there were immediate answers.

I was suspicious of such a ministry. These weren't Christians at all. This was probably a front for the Reagan administration to draw gays out of the closet in order to track the AIDS epidemic. But I wrote to the ministry anyway.

I received a call from Jim, a ministry leader. He encouraged me and prayed with me. He invited me to my first meeting. Unfortunately, it was the same night in which the group was having a wake for a group member who died of AIDS.

That Friday I arrived at the church forty minutes early and drove back and forth again and again, debating whether or not to go in. Finally, I drove into the church lot and parked behind a huge tree so that my car would not be visible from the road. Who could tell! Reagan operatives could be concealed across the street using telephoto lenses.

I went in and immediately knew I had forgotten something: ten milligrams of Valium. I knew I would faint. Here I was, among a group of people who were potential partners, and I was going to come out of the closet, and out of the life, in the same evening.

We sat in a circle and began singing hymns, not solid 300-year-old Presbyterian hymns, but upbeat, charismatic-style worship songs. O God! They're clapping, they're going to lay hands on my head next and pronounce me delivered. What am I doing here? After twenty minutes I stood up and headed for the door. "I just can't," I said twice, and melodramatically sashayed out with a Bette Davis flair.

FATHER, I AM NO LONGER WORTHY TO BE CALLED SON

I shook as I drove home, but halfway there I said to myself, "You are going back next week." And a peace descended upon me that passes all understanding. Scripture says, "But while he was still a long way off, his father saw him and was filled with compassion for him" (Luke 15:20).

UNDERSTANDING CAME FIRST

Friday night came at last. I arrived early so I could hide my car behind the tree again. "Lord," I prayed, "Get me through an entire evening, that's all I ask."

I stayed the whole evening, even though Bill told me later that he was certain I would never return. But praise God, I needed to hear what was said that evening. God wanted me to hear it.

That evening confirmed for me that the Lord always ministers to us in the way that we need. He appreciated and knew my skeptical, cynical nature. He also knew of my profound intellectual and inquisitive mind. He knew I needed more than a rousing hymn. I needed to understand first.

After the hymn, Dr. Bill, the ministry director, gave a lesson on the development of the homosexual problem. It was an academic and factual description of how homosexual feelings arise from the unfulfilled relationship of a boy with his father and/or men.

I was ecstatic. I wished I had brought a notebook to take notes in, but I hung on every word. And the most important message I needed to hear was, I wasn't born that way, therefore change is possible. Homosexuality was nothing more than the symptom of an emotionally wounded personality, said Dr. Bill.

After a while I felt as if I were the only person in the room and Bill was speaking to me personally. Low self-esteem leads to gender emptiness, which leads to gender attraction, which leads to sexual attraction, reinforcement, and homosexual identification.

As he described each step of the development, I wanted to scream out "Yes! yes!" for I could identify the feelings of each of the stages he was describing. Then Bill said one thing that solidified my determination. It was unintentional, but I believe the Lord let me hear it in a way that would prompt action. Bill said that once the homosexual behavior is secured through reinforcement, change after age thirty-five becomes very difficult. The reason for this is that around age thirty-five people are consolidating and settling their life goals and identity for the rest of their lives.

EARLY SIGNS OF CHANGE
Two of the immediate signs of the Lord's blessings were an end to my use of alcohol and my outrageous character. Weeks went by. I studied; I read; I learned as much as I could. I prayed. But I noticed when I was strung out or stressed or tired, still I became tempted. Two falls followed. One was my last sexual encounter with Jimmy. It cost me $100.

I called Bill. He walked me through what had happened. It was so clear. I was angry after getting stuck with the dinner tab for two other men from the ministry. I became defiant and used the sexual outlet to reduce my anxiety. My wounded area, as Bill calls it, was aggravated and I felt that complex of sensitive and painful emotions which leaves me empty and deprived. These are the dynamics that happen just before a fall.

THE INTERNAL WORK DEEPENS

I began a retreat about then. Not prayer exactly, but conversations with the Lord. Several nights a week, I would get in the car and drive. I spoke out loud, talking with the child inside who had been so hurt. Events which happened thirty years ago started to come up from my burial ground and became clear. I relived the teasing I received from the boys in the neighborhood. I saw how I had become a pawn in my mother's need to be a good parent. I saw vividly how the silence from my father caused me to feel his rejection and resulted in that broken love bond between us.

One night was particularly revealing. As I drove, the question came out of my mouth before I was even conscious of it. It leaped from my unconscious burial ground. "Daddy, Daddy, why, why, why didn't you, couldn't you just have said it once—that you loved me? When I came home bloodied from the neighborhood kids, couldn't you say you were proud of me? Couldn't you say that you accepted me? Why, Daddy, why not just once?" Anger, pain, the need for his love, grieving; I was reliving it all.

I had to pull the car over. I cried for nearly an hour. Every frustration came to the surface in a kaleidoscope of horror. "Mommy, will you love me if I'm not perfect? And, for God's sake, why couldn't you encourage me for what I am? Why did you keep me so rigid that I couldn't be my own person? Can you ever let go?" Oh, this is so painful to think about and write about!

TAKE NOTICE!

People started to ask if I lost weight (I had gained weight); if I bought new clothes, new glasses, dyed my hair, or even if I had been to a tanning studio. Something was showing.

I was at dinner at Bill and Louise's house; two wonderful people whom God provided as my "special friends." After a couple of hours of casual conversation, Bill went right to the point. "OK, what's going on, David? What's her name?" I said, "What do you mean?" "I don't know," he replied, "the last three or four months, you have become more distinguished."

What a word to use. It was a wonderful word for how I was

feeling. "No, Bill," I said, "it's not a new woman in my life. I have been in a support group. You see. Well, I am . . . was . . . homosexual, and I'm trying to get out."

The pause was deafening. I wanted to run away, die, make a joke, anything to diffuse the horror of that silent moment. "We had thought that that might be the case," Bill said, "but we were never sure. We just want you to know that it doesn't matter to us, if you are straight or gay." Louise got up, came over and hugged me. "You know we love you, David, no matter what." No matter what, these two people loved me and accepted me. No strings. No conditions. Why couldn't they have been Mommy and Daddy?

HEALING IS A PROCESS THAT TAKES TIME

At the end of my first year of recovery, I attended the Exodus International Conference. I met hundreds of other Christian ex-gay men and women at various stages of recovery. I met people out of the life for years. It was all confirmation that the process I was going through was not a game or a fantasy, but reality. Homosexuals can and do change.

I am never going to return to my former life of depravity, sin, and self-destruction. In my role as counselor and teacher in HOPE Ministries, I learn and grow each time I am asked to help someone else. It is now over two years since I attended my first HOPE meeting. This has been a time of bitterness, anger, rage, depression, fear, and confusion that I would not have endured if I had known it ahead of time. I am moving through those stages of change and integration. I am coming closer to a time of greater self-acceptance. I am seeing the spiritual opportunities which all this work has given me. I am seeing more clearly the hand of God in all of this. Praise God, "He who began a good work," is completing it, in His way and in His own timing.

Homosexual feelings are little more than a nuisance to me most of the time now. I have slips and backslidings and I cave in to my stress-relief cycle periodically. Sure, occasionally I see a man who turns my head. The yearning, lustful desire rises up occasionally. Yet the thought of sexual involvement with a guy now is almost as repellent as it would be for any heterosexual man. It seems silly, abnormal, stupid, and strange. It's a lie and a deception, and I can see it as such.

As for women, no, I haven't started dating, but I have become an incurable flirt at the grocery store. I feel the security to take those risks with women. I am anxious to date, but I'll wait for the Lord's timing on this. I describe myself in terms of dating, as a thirty-eight-year-old with a sixteen-year-old outlook. That gap between my chronological and emotional age is closing very quickly. I know dating will not be easy. I know I have a fear and a barrier to women I must overcome. In His time! In His time!

My parents are healing too. They have had to go through a great deal of grief and guilt, which I know has been difficult for them. My mom is changing her controlling and manipulative behavior with me, even though at times she can still set me up with frustration, discouragement, and anger. Dad is becoming more openly affectionate in word and deed.

I lost thirty-five pounds, and work out at a gym now. I have passed the ultimate test of recovery — engaging in casual conversation in a locker room with a naked man while maintaining eye contact. But, thank God, all things work together for good for the one who loves God and is called according to His purpose. Thank You, Jesus, thank You!

FOR THE COUNSELOR

These last words are just for you, the counselor. I want to minister to you. And once again, I come back to my verse: Romans 8:28. I encourage you to make it your verse also. If you believe it with all your heart, you will never fail in your work with overcomers, for look at what it says.

We know that all things work. However stationary and indiscernable this journey seems at times to your overcomer, it is obvious that God continues to work in him and in his life, and through you. There have been many times when you will see no progress; no movement; no change in your overcomer. You, the counselor, may become discouraged. Then the Lord steps in once again and you can see that He has been working all the time. He continues to work. He never slumbers or sleeps. The unseen seed in the ground, day and night, continues to grow. First the blade, then the ear, finally the ripe wheat suitable for harvesting.

We know that all things work together. Your overcomer will feel that he is in a state of contradiction and contrast. He is hot and cold; up and down; clear and confused; eager and unmotivated; believing and disbelieving. You may feel the same at times as you go through the changes with him.

But there is a harmony working itself out in all the things that are happening. Like the many cogs and wheels of a great piece of machinery or the delicate, precise movements of a fine watch, all things are working together. During times of setbacks and slipups you may wonder if it all makes any sense. But the Wise Physician, the Good Shepherd, puts one thing together with a second thing, and then a third and a fourth, and all of these together work unto good.

We know that all things work together for good. God is good. He is Goodness. He gave His Son; can He withhold any good thing? He is good; can He give anything except what are good and perfect gifts? He is love; can He permit anything harmful to those who love Him; to those who have been purchased by the blood of His Son? When your overcomer looks at the road he has followed, can't he see that all God's dealings with him in the past have been designed for his good?

We know that all things work together for good for the one who loves God and is called according to His purpose. God always had a purpose in what He was doing in calling you to the work of healing with overcomers. All He needs from you is your faithful love and obedience. This is the only condition you and your overcomer must fulfill. Pause with me now and let these words of God penetrate and saturate you with faith as you continue the good work to which you have been called.

"Let us hold unswervingly to the hope we profess, for He who promised is faithful" (Heb. 10:23).

"The Lord is faithful, and He will strengthen and protect you from the evil one" (2 Thes. 3:3).

"Your faithfulness continues through all generations" (Ps. 119:90).

"Remember Your word to Your servant, for You have given me hope" (Ps. 119:49).

"But by faith we eagerly await through the Spirit the

wholeness for which we hope" (Gal. 5:5).

"When you pass through the waters, I will be with you. . . . When you walk through the fire, you will not be burned; the flames will not set you ablaze. . . . For I am the Lord your God, the Holy One of Israel, your Savior. Do not be afraid, for I am with you" (Isa. 43:2-3, 5).

Let us pray:

Father, I thank You for calling me to this ministry of healing. I thank You, Father, that You have prepared my life and my mind, my inner parent, my inner child, and my inner adult, to understand this homosexual woundedness.

Father, I thank You that You have performed a healing in my own life, so that I would be able to understand and feel the pain of others.

Father, I praise You for the words You have inspired in this book. I ask that You take these words and impress them upon the hearts and minds of those who read them. Let Your Holy Spirit enter deeply into the burial ground of pain for anyone reading this book. Let your Spirit reveal and heal that fearful, hiding child, embrace that critical and rejecting parent, and strengthen that voice of his inner adult.

Father, I thank You for David. I thank You for his healing. I thank You for all those who have received healing by this ministry. Knowing that "all things work together for good," I thank You, I praise You, in the precious, beautiful, powerful name of Your Son, JESUS! Amen.

GLOSSARY OF TERMS

Addictive homosexuality: Continuous, frequent, and repetitive homosexual behavior or acting out of homosexuality. Not all or even most overcomers engage in addictive homosexuality.

Acting out: Homosexual behavior or actual homosexual activities, in contrast to the emotional disorientation.

AIDS: Acquired Immunodeficiency Syndrome is a viral infectious transmitted sexual disease common to homosexuals though also transmitted by needles shared by intravenous drug users.

Born again: The new spiritual birth which results from accepting the Lord Jesus Christ as Savior. This is also known as being saved or salvation. A born-again person has a spiritually alive heart. The Holy Spirit has quickened or given life to his human spirit. He has God's own life in him. He is a new creation in Christ Jesus.

Boulders, rocks, pebbles: The analogy of the stream of sexuality and the obstacles that prevent the normal development of heterosexuality. Major boulders are low self-esteem and gender identity insecurity.

Broken love-bond: The defective emotional connectedness with the parent of the same gender which develops into gender identity insecurity or gender emptiness. For various reasons in himself and in his relationship with his same-sex parent, the child is unable to identify with and assume a secure same-gender self-image.

Burial ground: The "place" in the unconscious (heart or human spirit) of the person where childhood emotional memories, fears, fixed ideas, impressions, anxieties, sins, wounds, and hurts remain active and unresolved. The place where the wounded area is located which keeps homosexuality alive.

Changed heart: The renewal of the human spirit or unconscious when the Holy Spirit comes to dwell in a person who is born again. Interchangeable with the idea of salvation.

Challenges of the heart: The continual spiritual exercise of faith, hope, and love toward God that produces a transformed life in Christ. Interchangeable with sanctification.

Choices of the heart: The exercise of spiritual practices which flow from a changed heart. These include prayer, worship, fellowship, Bible study, and daily conversations with the Lord.

Christ in you: The presence and power of Christ's Spirit in the born-again person. In the saved person, Christ's Spirit (the Holy Spirit) works through the mature inner adult voice within the personality to transform and renew the whole person. See John 15:4; Romans 8:10-11; 2 Corinthians 4:10; 13:5; Galatians 2:20; Ephesians 2:4-5; 3:17; Philippians 1:21; Colossians 1:27.

Compulsive personality: Very common among overcomers; it is an inclination to perfectionistic standards of behavior, i.e., neatness, ritualism, organization, rigidity, and control. Often the result of a childhood in which emotions were difficult to express as part of a dysfunctional family.

Consciousness: That aspect of personality that is part of the soul; the person's awareness of outer reality (body, others, the world around him) and inner reality (feelings, thoughts, and motives). In psychology, it describes a well functioning "ego" or ability to perceive reality in non-distorted ways.

Conspiracy of factors theory: The multiple factors which contribute to the development of homosexuality; includes pre-birth and post-birth contributors.

Conversations with the Lord: One of three inner conversations which needs changing in order to effect inner healing. Often the overcomer has distorted conversations with the Lord due to his inaccurate view of God as unapproachable, judgmental, and punitive.

Conversations with the inner parent: One of three inner conversations which needs changing in order to effect inner healing. These inner conversations originated from childhood experiences with his parents. They now arise when "transferences" are made to others who stimulate his parental voice. Six areas of transferences are power, judgmentalism, eroticism, superiority-inferiority, dependency, and intimacy.

Conversations with the inner child: One of three inner

conversations which needs changing in order to effect inner healing. These conversations distort, deny, or disregard the overcomer's feelings, and are changed by the four steps of emotional renewal.

Cruising: The activity among homosexuals of driving through known areas where "gays" arrange sexual encounters with each other. Cruising areas are often parks, highway rest stops, parking lots, and other hangouts.

Deprivation complex: Also known as the "wounded area": the "place" within the unconscious burial ground where the broken love-bond with the parent of the same gender became lodged, and where the fifteen wounded needles continue to stimulate emotional pain leading to homosexual acting out.

Devitalization: The depleted, defeated state of emotional emptiness which is chronic in overcomers.

Disorientation: Or "homosexual disorientation": the way in which God-given heterosexuality became sidetracked because of the emotional barriers in childhood and adolescence.

Dysfunctional family: The typical family environment of overcomers in which feelings were unacknowledged and unacceptable, leading to LSE and GE.

Emotional dependency (or ED): An exaggerated attachment and need for another characterized by obsessiveness, jealousy, fear of loss, and lack of emotional separation. ED is emotionally unhealthy and spiritually arresting.

Emotional renewal (Four Steps): The four steps recommended to overcomers to heal the sensitive inner child voice. They are (1) Name it; (2) Face it, feel it; (3) Talk it, talk to it; and (4) Act it, act on it.

External changes: One major dimension of healing homosexuality involving seven personal and relational changes, including the five homosexual outlets.

Gay: The term used among the general population to describe homosexuality as an alternative and equal sexual preference to heterosexuality.

Gender attraction: The third stage of homosexual development usually before adolescence when the child begins to feel an emotional and physical attraction to a same-gender person, though not yet in eroticized ways.

Gender emptiness (or GE): The critical second stage of homosexual development during which the child experiences gender confusion and alienation or gender identity insecurity.

Gender identity insecurity: Synonymous with gender emptiness.

Gender identity security: An emotional and social confidence of one's gender identity which matches one's anatomical sex.

H.A.B.I.T.: The five strategies to break the habit of masturbation or other sexual temptations. An acronym for Hazardous situation, Actions, Bible verses, Intentions, and Thoughts.

Heart: The unconscious in psychology. The human spirit or deepest dimension of the personality according to the Bible.

HIV: Human Immunodeficiency Virus; the common term used to describe the AIDS virus.

Homoemotional: A term used by Dr. Elizabeth Moberly which describes the normal emotional needs in same-gender relationships and emphasizes the underlying nonsexual needs in same-gender bonding.

Homosexuality: Sexual interest in and strong emotional attachment to a person of the same sex.

Homosexual identity: The last or sixth stage of homosexual development in which the person resolves his sexual "orientation" privately (and perhaps publicly) by accepting himself as exclusively homosexual.

Homosexual obsession: An emotional obsession for the attention, acceptance, and love of a same-gender person. An unresolved, homoemotional hunger for intimacy with the same sex.

Homosexual outlets: Five basic ways in which homosexuality is enacted. (1) Emotional dependency and longing for intimacy, (2) Sexual encounters, (3) Pornography, (4) Masturbation, and (5) Visual indulgence. When an overcomer has greatly diminished or eliminated these five outlets (in combination with other internal healing), he is considered substantially healed.

Homosexual reinforcement (or HR): The fifth stage of homosexual development in which the person develops behavioral patterns through repetition of 'homosexual outlets, fantasies, and thinking.

Inner voices: The three inner voices that need changing to effect inner healing: inner adult, inner parent, inner child.

Inner parent: Or critical inner parent voice. One of the three voices the overcomer has internalized from the actual, often negative, conversations he has had with his real parent(s).

Inner child: Or sensitive inner child voice. One of the three voices the overcomer has internalized from his childhood memories of negative, painful, and unresolved feelings (the fifteen needles), which continue to stimulate homosexuality.

Inner adult: Or mature inner adult voice. One of the three inner voices. For the saved person, the voice through which the Spirit of Christ speaks to the other two voices. Interior healing is substantially affected as the overcomer yields to this Spirit-led voice within him.

Internal changes: Removing the boulders, rocks, and pebbles by improving self-esteem, gender identity security, spiritual renewal, self-acceptance, and improving interior self-talk.

Masturbation: The intentional stimulation of the genitals to arouse sexual excitement and pleasure for the purpose of reaching orgasm.

Needles: The fifteen troublesome emotions in the unconscious that make up the wounded area or deprivation complex. Like sharp needles, these emotions continue to stab the overcomer when they are experienced.

Opposite sex intimacy anxiety: Unpleasant physical and emotional sensations that inhibit physical and emotional closeness with a person of the opposite sex.

Overcomer: The term used throughout this book for the Christian struggling to overcome homosexuality. It is used in contrast to the world's terms for one who accepts his homosexuality, such as "homosexual" or "gay."

Personality anatomy: The elements of personality, including the body (physical senses), the soul (consciousness, self-consciousness), and the human spirit (unconscious or heart).

Paradoxical results: A technique to reduce temptation by exaggerating the idealized characteristics of a person one is attracted to in order to realize the false idol one has made of that person. See Romans 1:22-27.

Porcupine guards: An analogy for the way the overcomer protects his sensitive wounded emotions (needles) by acting like a porcupine that sends out protective, defensive needles when he feels threatened. Fight, flight, and fright reactions are typical.

Predisposing factors: The pre-birth factors which may make a person vulnerable to homosexuality such as chromosomal complexities, in-utero trauma, or a sensitive temperament. Though these may be present, they neither cause homosexuality alone or together, nor are they irreversible. Rather, homosexuality is predominantly a response to post-birth factors in the family.

Proactive: Or, doing what is "right." An important concept of making positive, constructive, and forceful responses to the wounded emotions instead of reacting defensively and protectively.

Protective reactions (Guards): See porcupine guards.

Pseudovitalization: The false and fleeting sense of relief that the overcomer feels when he has engaged in some homosexual acting out. It is a temporary substitute and stress reducer in the stress-relief cycle.

Reorientation therapy: The approach to recovery of heterosexuality outlined in this book based on the analogy of the stream of heterosexuality.

Satan cycle: An emotional cycle of lust, indulgence, self-condemnation, discouragement, depression, hopelessness common to overcomers. Satan is victorious if he can discourage the overcomer.

Self-consciousness: One's self-image and self-esteem.

Self-esteem: The way a person "feels" about himself. His sense of self-significance, self-security, self-worth.

Self-image: The way a person "thinks" about himself, often based on his characteristics and roles in life and the way others see him.

Setups: The people, events, or circumstances that stimulate the wounded area or deprivation complex.

Spoil or break the idol: A technique used to diminish temptation by which the overcomer reminds himself of some "cold" and realistic facts about the person to whom he is attracted.

Stages of integration: Five stages of integration through which the overcomer must go in order to experience substantial healing: (1) Anger/discouragement/self-rejection, (2) Acceptance of the struggle, (3) Acceptance of himself as more than "homosexual," (4) Self-acceptance of himself more completely as this unique person, (5) Spiritual embracing of the homosexual struggle in peace and thankfulness (Rom. 8:28).

Stream of heterosexuality: The analogy used to describe the flow of heterosexuality as God designed it. Homosexuality is a deviation from the flow due to barriers in the heterosexual stream.

Stress-relief cycle: The common way in which overcomers experience and manage stress, leading to homosexual acting out.

Symbolic questioning: A technique used to diminish temptation by which the overcomer recognizes that the attractive characteristics are symbols of what he wants for himself.

Transferences: The tendency to habitually perceive and react to others in ways learned from childhood in relation to one's parents.

Triggers: Anything that directly stimulates sexual excitement or arousal, e.g., pornography, gay bars, cruising areas, rest rooms, etc.

Two-week challenge: A strategy used to break the cycle of addictive masturbation by which the overcomer commits himself to abstain for two weeks as a contract made with his counselor.

RECOMMENDED READING LIST

Books on Homosexuality
Beyond Rejection by Don Baker. A well-written story of a married man's struggle with homosexuality, and how his wife and pastor deal with the situation (Multnomah, 1985).

Homosexuality: Laying the Axe to the Roots by Ed Hurst. A gem of a booklet. Hurst looks at nine underlying sin issues ("roots") that give rise to the surface symptom of homosexual temptation (Multnomah).

Pursuing Sexual Wholeness: How Jesus Heals the Homosexual by Andrew Comiskey. Based on the author's "Living Waters" group program, this book provides rich new insights into the "bigger picture" of homosexual healing (Creation House, 1989).

You Don't Have to Be Gay by J.A. Konrad. A collection of letters from a Christian ex-gay to his unsaved friend. Konrad's warmth complements a clear explanation of the homosexual condition and change process. The book is evangelistic without being offensive, with a powerful potential for reaching unsaved readers. Warning: Occasional swear words and sexual slang may offend some readers (Pacific Publishing House, 1987).

Steps Out of Homosexuality by Frank Worthen. An extremely practical book for men desiring freedom from homosexuality. Also excellent for pastors and counselors (Regeneration Books).

Books on Lesbianism
Beyond the Wall by Carrie Wingfield. Carrie shares how Jesus freed her from homosexuality (Regeneration Books).

Long Road to Love by Darlene Bogle. The testimony of a former lesbian. Her struggle to extricate herself from a deeply ingrained immoral lifestyle is well-described (Chosen Books/Revell, 1985).

Books on Relationships
Emotional Dependency: A Threat to Close Friendships by Lori

T. Rentzel. A superb booklet for dealing with friendships which have become too close. Contains insights applicable to all relationships, not solely homosexual (Regeneration Books, 1984).

The Friendships of Women by Dee Brestin. Through scriptural models and contemporary examples, the author portrays friendships as God intends them to be (Victor Books, 1988).

Books for Counselors
The Broken Image by Leanne Payne. Ideal for counselors who want to know more about inner healing and how it specifically applies to the homosexual problem. The material is scholarly in content, but is written from the vantage point of years of experience by the author (Crossway Books, 1981).

Homosexuality: A New Christian Ethic by Elizabeth Moberly. This book shows how the proper development of same-sex friendships is a vital step of healing from homosexuality. Helpful conclusions drawn from this psychologist's many years of research (Attic Press, 1983).

Books for Friends and Family
Parents in Pain by John White. Help for dealing with traumatic family situations (InterVarsity, 1979).

Where Does a Mother Go to Resign? by Barbara Johnson. A mother's story of surviving tragedy: the disablement of her husband, deaths of two sons, and the discovery of another son's homosexuality (Bethany House, 1979). Also see Johnson's other two excellent books, *Fresh Elastic for Stretched-Out Moms* (Fleming Revell, 1986), and *Stick a Geranium in Your Hat* (Word, 1990).

Related Reading—Key Issues in Christian Growth
How to Say No to a Stubborn Habit by Erwin Lutzer. A great help in resisting sexual temptations (Victor Books, 1986). Also see *Living with Your Passions* (Victor Books, 1983).

Inside Out by Larry Crabb. Crabb zeroes in on the core of human problems with insights applicable to sexually related problems. It's also good for gently deflating the "no one understands" mind-set of many homosexual strugglers (NavPress, 1988).

AIDS

The AIDS Epidemic—Balancing Compassion and Justice by Glenn Wood, M.D. and John Dietrich, M.D. One of the finest Christian books on AIDS to date. Topics cover a wide gamut, from a readable medical overview to the church's responsibility to persons with AIDS. The authors uphold a biblical standard against sin while demonstrating compassion to those who suffer its consequences (Multnomah, 1990).

How Will I Tell My Mother? by Jerry Arterburn. Jerry shares his struggles in facing death from AIDS, and telling his family about his homosexuality (Thomas Nelson, 1988).